What th[...]
Are Sayi[...]
TEENS SPEAK OUT . . .

Somewhere I saw a quote that concluded, "Common sense is not very common." In our day, biblical obedience is even less common. Yet followers of Jesus Christ, whether old or young, are called to precisely that uncommon obedience. Josh calls young people to the only answer to today's sexually driven dilemmas — obedience. I recommend this book heartily.

Jay Kesler, President, Taylor University

An unusually enlightening resource . . . we needed this revealing information decades ago. This is must reading for all parents and every person in ministry.

H. Norman Wright, Professor, Therapist, Author

It is shocking how many of our young people — even those in our best churches — are sexually active (more than 50 percent). Yet many said, "I really did not want to; I was 'pressured.' " For months I've thought that someone should write a book to encourage them to say NO! and instruct them HOW TO SAY NO! Josh has done it so well that I won't have to. Every parent and teen should read this book.

Tim LaHaye, President, Family Life Seminars

We've waited too long for a "Why Wait?" program. Thanks, Josh, for stepping out and taking the lead. Your resources are what we need to rescue kids out of the sexual slaughterhouse. Terrific tools!

Chuck Klein, National Director, Student Venture

A truth shocker for every parent of teens! This book opens the window and lets a bright light shine in on a subject we've kept in the shadows. Teens themselves revealing, in their own candid style, their personal sexual struggles and the reasons, peel back the layers of religious skepticism that keep us from seeing how the sexual revolution has invaded the church youth group. These facts will certainly surprise, possibly startle, and clearly set forth a solution of positive action ideas.

Dr. J. Allen Petersen, Family Concern

Josh McDowell has done a superb job of alerting the church to a problem that has reached epidemic proportions. Based on interviews with hundreds of Christian kids, this book documents the extent of teenage promiscuity. But it does more. It shows realistically why kids should wait for sex, and it gives practical guidelines to help young people control their galloping sexual urges.

Gary R. Collins, Trinity Evangelical Divinity School

Here is a book I would encourage every teenager and parent to read. *Teens Speak Out: What I Wish My Parents Knew About My Sexuality* is an honest, open statement of what is going on sexually among our Christian teenagers today. But best of all this book provides sound, tested answers to this astounding problem — both for the teenager and for the parents. My profound prayer for our teenagers is that they will be able to cope with the pressures of premarital sex, and this book will help in this critical task.

D. Ross Campbell, M.D.

An Awareness Book

This book, *Teens Speak Out,* is the first in a series of publications included in the national "Why Wait?" campaign, a multi-media effort to help parents and teens stem the tide of the sexual crisis engulfing our culture today. *Teens Speak Out* is comprised primarily of hundreds of responses from the teenagers themselves indicating what they are thinking and feeling.

The purpose of this book is to awaken and inform adults about the problems and pressures teenagers are facing. Other books and tapes in the series will provide much more in the way of information, understanding and direction as they deal with these issues and what can be done about them.

Ask your Christian bookseller for these titles:

- *Why Wait? What You Need To Know About the Teen Sexuality Crisis*
- *The Secret of Loving*
  (by Josh McDowell)
- *Dating: Picking (and Being) a Winner*
- *Sex: Desiring the Best*
- *Love: Making It Last*
  (by Barry St. Clair and Bill Jones, Josh McDowell — Series Editor)

The publishers

♥ ♥ ♥

JOSH McDOWELL

WHY WAIT?

TEENS SPEAK OUT:

"What I Wish My Parents Knew About My Sexuality"

Here's Life Publishers

Published by
HERE'S LIFE PUBLISHERS, INC.
P.O. Box 1576
San Bernardino, CA 92402

HLP Product Number 951616
©1987, Josh McDowell
All rights reserved.
Printed in the United States of America

Library of Congress Cataloging-in-Publication Data

McDowell, Josh.
    What I wish my parents knew about my sexuality.

    1. Youth — United States — Sexual behavior. 2. Sex
instruction for youth — United States — Religious
aspects — Christianity. 3. Youth — Family relationships.
4. Youth — Psychology. I. Title.
HQ35.M4 1987   306.7'088055   86-22759
ISBN 0-89840-168-2 (pbk.)

Scripture references are taken from the following versions of the Bible and are identified accordingly: New International Version — NIV; New American Standard Bible, — NASB; King James Version — KJV.

FOR MORE INFORMATION, WRITE:

L.I.F.E. — P.O. Box A399, Sydney South 2000, Australia
Campus Crusade for Christ of Canada — Box 300, Vancouver, B.C. V6C 2X3, Canada
Campus Crusade for Christ — Pearl Assurance House, 4 Temple Row, Birmingham, B2 5HG, England
Lay Institute for Evangelism — P.O. Box 8786, Auckland 3, New Zealand
Great Commission Movement of Nigeria — P.O. Box 500, Jos, Plateau State Nigeria, West Africa
Campus Crusade for Christ International — Arrowhead Springs, San Bernardino, CA 92414, U.S.A.

FIRST PRINTING, MARCH 1987
SECOND PRINTING, JULY 1987
THIRD PRINTING, AUGUST 1987
FOURTH PRINTING, SEPTEMBER 1987
FIFTH PRINTING, NOVEMBER 1987
SIXTH PRINTING, FEBRUARY 1988

To all the teens who "wrote their hearts out."
This is their book. They wrote it and they deserve the
credit.

Acknowledgments

I want to acknowledge all the work Matt and Claudia Judge did in compiling the essays into manuscript form. Without their efforts the finished product would have taken so much longer.

CONTENTS

SECTION I
"What's Going On In My World"

SECTION II
"How You Can Guide Me Through My World"

SECTION III
Sex: To Have or Not To Have

SECTION IV
Essays: Writing Their Hearts Out

SECTION I
"What's Going On In My World"

1

Teens Speak Out

How we found out what they're really thinking.

— ♥ —

This is a book no adult is qualified to write. To truly understand the needs of today's youth on an intimate level, to comprehend their fears, their questions, the pressures they feel, a person must be one of them. I do not qualify.

Though countless teenagers long to communicate with their parents about the struggles they face in a world obsessed by sex, few find they are able to. Fewer still would dream of attempting to write a book about teenagers and their sexuality.

Therefore, it was necessary to work together with teens on this project. The young people supplied the information. I simply am passing it along.

What you are about to read has come from four main sources:

1. *Questionnaires,* to be answered anonymously, were distributed at Operation Sonshine, a week of training and evangelism at Daytona Beach, Florida, sponsored by Campus Crusade for Christ. The survey asked four personal questions about sexual activity the

respondent may have been involved in since becoming a Christian, and the consequences of this activity.

More than six hundred such surveys were returned, many with extra pages attached. The stories told of physical, emotional and spiritual damage done by premarital sex, and were so painful that I couldn't read many of them at one sitting.

A great number of these responses showed intense personal insight into the causes and results of their activity, and the blanket of anonymity allowed an honesty not always possible in discussions with other Christians.

2. *Personal and group interviews* have been conducted by research associates with hundreds of high school and college students in many different parts of the country, and the students' responses were recorded.

3. *Response sheets* were passed out at churches and youth group meetings and schools where I spoke. These sheets contained the simple question, What would you like to say to your parents (in fifty words or less)?

4. *Essays* were entered in a "Write Your Heart Out" contest, sponsored by the Josh McDowell Ministry. We asked people ages 12 to 30 to answer questions about premarital sex. One question was, What would you like to tell your parents about your sexuality? Much of this book is taken from the almost ten thousand pages submitted in the essay contest.

The book contains a mixture of opinions and insight about premarital sex and relationships from those closest to the battle. The methods used in gathering these thoughts were different, and the nature of the responses shifts from person to person. Some of the responses are very emotional; some are analytical. Some deal with inner struggles; some deal with societal changes. Some were written spontaneously; some were written only after much consideration. Some relate the joys and victories in the person's life; others relate painful hurts and deep frustrations. Some address parents directly, but most simply relate personal situations.

Regardless of the style or perspective, all of these come from the heart. I have sorted everything into chapters, and the punctuation and grammar have been polished — but the messages are intact.

Most of the responses have come from teenagers and young adults, but some came from older adults reflecting back on their youth.

Do you understand the struggles your children are going through? I have discovered that they really want you to understand. Imagine the pain of the 15-year-old who wrote, "My parents don't know who I am because they haven't taken the time to find out."

The fact that you are reading this means you have at least some degree of interest in knowing what teenagers want to say to their parents concerning their sexuality. What you read may surprise you or even shock you (although no explicit language is used or intimate scenes described). See how you feel after reading the following excerpt from one essay:

> Yes, even though I am a Christian 18-year-old girl, I feel pressures. Where some people get the idea that Christian teenage girls feel no pressures is beyond me. It seems the stereotypes are that girls are supposed to be the ones who say NO because girls don't feel much. Maybe I am not like average girls, but I don't find it easy to say NO.
>
> Lately . . . I have gone out only with Christians and I have had little pressure from them, but we still have desires and the pressure is there. There is pressure from society and pressure from peers, but I feel the pressure for sex within myself and there

JOSH McDOWELL invites you to...

Write Your Heart Out WHY WAIT?

1986 Magnavox Large Screen TV, Camera and Video Cassette Recorders top the array of fabulous prizes.

"I can't remember a project I've been more excited about than this effort to tell the truth about premarital sex. Everyone who takes the time to enter will be a winner in his or her own life. I hope you will win one of these prizes too!"

Josh

1985 NATIONAL ESSAY CONTEST on PREMARITAL SEX
$40,000 in PRIZES for individuals and groups

Involvement in premarital sex is scarring the lives of millions of people. To meet the problem head-on, Josh McDowell has undertaken a major project called "Why Wait?" Its purpose is to reveal the very best reasons and ways for saying "no" to premarital sex. You are urged to speak your heart in this unique essay contest. If you wish you can remain anonymous. Whether you win a prize, or not you will receive rich personal rewards as you write your heart out.

3 ENTRY AGE CATEGORIES

Individuals and/or groups in these three age categories may submit essay contest entries (Age on entry deadline, March 1, 1986):

Category A: Ages 12 to 15
Category B: Ages 16 to 19
Category C: Ages 20 to 30

10 PRIZES IN EACH CATEGORY

A guaranteed total of 30 prizes worth a total of $40,000 will be awarded to both individuals and the groups they represent. Twenty prizes will be identical in each category, with one exception. The individual first prize in Category C is a Caribbean Christian cruise.

	INDIVIDUAL	GROUP
1ST	$1,500.00 Cash	Magnavox 37" large screen TV, Video Cassette Recorder with Remote Control and Lolite Video Camera
2ND	$1,000.00 Cash	Expense-paid, one-day visit by Josh McDowell to your group
3RD	$500 Cash	Magnavox Video Cassette Recorder with Remote Control

Runner Up Prizes include a variety of Josh McDowell film series rentals, books and audio cassette tapes.

THE ESSAYS

Each separate essay entry must concentrate on one of the following topics:

1. *Explain the reasons people in your age category become sexually active before marriage.*
2. *Discuss why you agree or disagree with this statement: A person should wait until marriage to engage in sex.*
3. *Tell what you wish your parents understood about your sexuality and the pressures you feel about engaging in premarital sex.*
4. *Offer the advice you would put in a letter to an unmarried friend who is sexually involved.*
5. *Describe the ways you and others have been pressured to have premarital sex, and give the most effective answers when this happens.*

Individuals or groups of individuals working together may submit as many essays as they wish. To be accepted, essays must be typed, double-spaced, on unlined white paper, and no more than 2,000 words in length and identified by category according to the context rules.

Essays will be judged on originality, practicality, honesty, clarity, style, and sound use of biblical and psychological principles.

ENTER NOW BEFORE CONTEST DEADLINE:

Your essay(s) must be postmarked by midnight, March 1, 1986. Winners will be announced June 1, 1986. Address all entires to: Write Your Heart Out, P.O. Box 4248, San Diego, CA 92104.

PLEASE PHOTOCOPY THIS ANNOUNCEMENT AND DISTRIBUTE AS WIDELY AS POSSIBLE.

Please give to the youth worker in your church!

WHY WAIT?

JOSH McDOWELL ESSAY CONTEST RULES
"WRITE YOUR HEART OUT"
1985 NATIONAL ESSAY CONTEST ON PREMARITAL SEX

1. Entrants limited to individuals and/or groups of individuals in three age categories (age on entry deadline, March 1, 1986).

   Category A: Ages 12 to 15
   Category B: Ages 16 to 19
   Category C: Ages 20 to 30

2. Individual essay entries must concentrate on only one of the following topics. An individual or group may enter as many times as they wish.
   1. Explain the reasons people in your age category become sexually active before marriage.
   2. Discuss why you agree or disagree with this statement: A person should wait until marriage to engage in sex.
   3. Tell what you wish your parents understood about your sexuality and the pressures you feel about engaging in premarital sex.
   4. Offer the advice you would put in a letter to an unmarried friend who is sexually involved.
   5. Describe the ways you and others have been pressured to have premarital sex, and give the most effective answers when this happens.

3. Essays must be typed, double-spaced on white, unlined paper and be no more than 2,000 words in length.

4. A. Each page of the essay must be identified in the upper right hand corner with the:

      Author's name(s)
      Address
      Phone number
      Age category
      Sponsoring group name

   B. A 3 x 5 card with the above information must also be attached to the front of the essay.
   C. If an author chooses to remain anonymous, he or she must still provide a mailing address, phone number, age category and sponsoring group name.

5. The essays will be judged on originality, practicality, honesty, clarity, style and sound use of biblical and psychological principles.

6. A group writing effort by persons in the same age category is encouraged. Coaching by members of the same age category is therefore acceptable.

7. All entries must be postmarked by midnight, March 1, 1986. No exceptions will be made. Winners will be announced on June 1, 1986 and will be notified by certified mail.

8. All entries and their contents become the property of the Josh McDowell Ministry. No entry will be returned.

9. If used in any other part of the "Why Wait?" project, all names, dates and places mentioned in the essays and true stories they may contain will be changed.

(Post photocopies of these contest rules next to the poster or distribute to the members in your group to encourage participation.)

are no outlets in sight for this desire. Personally, I believe in the commandment of no sex before marriage, and I have kept it so far. I pray I won't break it if I meet a real charmer.

How do you feel about this young lady? After having counseled thousands of teenagers over the years, I would say that nothing in her experience is out of the ordinary. She has natural desires which, as she stated elsewhere in her essay, are a gift from God. She is open and honest about her feelings. She wants to stay on the right track with God, yet she's not quite sure who to turn to for guidance. She also wrote, "If my parents understood my pressures more, I feel I would be closer to them."

Christian young people often feel trapped in a cycle of struggle, guilt if they give in, and frustration at not being able to turn to their parents when they need words of wisdom or a sympathetic ear.

This is one reason we sponsored the essay contest. Yet some pastors and heads of Christian schools wrote to me and expressed shock that we would approach the subject of premarital sex. They seemed to feel that if we just ignore the concept of sexually active teenage Christians, there won't be any. Unfortunately, it's not that easy. Look at these figures:

- By the age of 19, 80 percent of the boys and 67 percent of the girls have had sex.
- There are more than 1 million teenage pregnancies every year.
- There are nearly 500,000 abortions performed on teenagers every year (one third of all abortions performed).
- More than 50 percent of the 21 million teens between the ages of 15 and 19 are sexually active.

And what about the church?

- Of 500 church youth surveyed, 62 percent said they had been involved in oral sex.
- Studies generally show that the percentage of sexually active Christian youth is about ten points behind the percentage of all teens. I estimate that between 55 and 60 percent of evangelical Christian youth are involved in sexual activity.
- A recent study commissioned by a major conservative evangelical denomination reported that within two years after graduation, 96 percent of their high school students leave the church. Less than 30 percent ever return.

I am convinced that premarital sexual activity is the *number one* hindrance to spiritual growth among the youth of this country.

As you read this material, you need to be aware of a couple of things. First, these are mostly teens speaking out. Their feelings and observations might not be an exact portrayal of the parent-teen situation. In some areas, you may begin to think that what these kids are feeling is not really valid, that there is no basis for their feelings or thoughts. We need to be reminded that whether our kids *should* feel that way or not isn't the issue. The issue is that they *do* feel that way, and that is reality to them, whether or not it is justifiable. You can argue with what they say . . . but you can't argue with what they feel.

One 13-year-old girl took a survey and this is her report:

When I asked a few boys about sex, here's what most of them said:
(1) Sex is one of the greatest things.

(2) Boys just can't live without sex.
(3) There's really nothing wrong with it.
(4) They think it feels so good.
(5) They also said all guys like it.

Now here are a few things some girls think that don't like sex:

(1) It's gonna be real scary the first time.
(2) There's too many risks in having it.
(3) That they might get too involved.
(4) They're afraid to lose their virginity.
(5) They might lose all feeling for each other.

Another thing you need to be aware of is that as you look at sexuality through the eyes of a young person, you can begin to feel inadequate and guilty, and you might even be thinking, *I've blown it. It's too late for my family. I've been a failure. I've let my kids down.*

Please believe me, with God's help it is never too late to begin to correct our failures. Authors Ray and Anne Ortlund very wisely point out it can't be too late...

as long as we're still alive. It's easy to think it's been too long to undo some wrong, but in God's economy, lost time seldom means permanent damage. In Joel 2:25 (NIV), God says, "I will repay you for the years that the locusts have eaten."

We didn't know a lot about raising kids when we had our oldest daughter, Sherry. We were her first parents and she was our first child! Of course there was tension. She is strong-willed and very bright. We did some crazy things, and probably what we did was totally wrong for her much of the time. But now our relationship is wonderful. We've gone through reconciliation after reconciliation, as all parents have to do, and today she and her husband, Walt, are among our closest friends. No, it is never too late to begin to correct failures.

We like these hymn words by Charles Wesley: "He breaks the power of canceled sin; He sets the prisoner free." No matter how many times we've repeated a bad habit in our parenting, God is more powerful than our sin. Grace is greater, and God is always ready to break that sin's power and start His gracious correction. Isn't God wonderful?[1]

"But, Josh, I get so discouraged. Sometimes I think nothing will work," you might say. When a child rebels, it's so easy to become discouraged. But, as author and mother Evelyn Christenson so aptly puts it,

We can counteract the effects of discouragement by keeping our eyes on God, and [continue] to trust Him. If a teen runs away from home, we need to keep our arms and our door open at all times.

Parents may want to kick the child out and be done with it because they are so discouraged. But I've learned never, never to give up. My brother turned his back on God when he was twenty. My mother and the rest of our family prayed for thirty years before he came back to God. That lesson in patience taught me to never give up on my children.

We need to replace our impatience over the teen's behavior with an absolute assurance that the child is going to come back. This may mean paying a costly price in disciplined prayer and letting the Lord change us. It's much easier to be disgruntled parents and just throw up our hands in defeat. But we need great strength to keep on interceding and undergirding the child in prayer.

No children do everything just the way parents want them to do. There were times when I was discouraged with my children. When that happened, I looked to God, not to the left or to the right, not to circumstances, not to myself, not to my own feelings. But I simply looked up to God and received assurance, comfort, and wisdom from Him.

In the end, no matter what the child does, we can still love him. We don't have to condone his behavior but we can continue to love the child because we want him in heaven with us. That's our ultimate goal in caring for our children.[2]

Dr. James Dobson gives a helpful insight to a parent's anxiety over past failures — and we've all had them. His years of dealing with parents in conferences and on a one-to-one basis have shown him:

There's hardly a parent alive who does not have some regrets and painful memories of failures as a mother or a father. Children are infinitely complex, and we cannot be perfect parents any more than we can be perfect human beings. The pressures of living are often enormous, and we get tired and irritated; we are influenced by our physical bodies and our emotions, which sometimes prevent us from saying the right things and being the model we should. We don't always handle our children as unemotionally as we wish we had, and it's very common to look back a year or two later and see how wrong we were in the way we approached a problem.

All of us experience these failures! *No one does the job perfectly!* That's why each of us should get alone with the Creator of parents and children, saying,

"Lord, You know my inadequacies. You know my weaknesses, not only in parenting, but in every area of my life. I did the best I could, but it wasn't good enough. As You broke the fishes and the loaves to feed the 5,000, now take my meager effort and use it to bless my family. Make up for the things I did wrong. Satisfy the needs that I have not satisfied. Wrap Your great arms around my children, and draw them close to You. And be there when they stand at the great crossroads between right and wrong. All I can give is my best, and I've done that. Therefore, I submit to You my children and myself and the job I did as a parent. The outcome now belongs to You."

I know God will honor that prayer, even for parents whose job is finished. The Lord does not want you to suffer from guilt over events you can no longer influence. The past is the past. Let it die, never to be resurrected.

Give the situation to God, and let Him have it. I think
you'll be surprised to learn that you're no longer alone![3]

Let me encourage you. It is never too late with
our children while we're still alive . . . no matter what
the age. There are times we have to admit our mistakes,
but we can learn from them and move on toward
building a better, healthier family relationship.

On the other hand, you could be saying, "I'm
doing such a good parenting job that this material
doesn't relate to me." One detriment to greatness is
satisfaction with the status quo. There are probably
more parents doing an excellent job of parenting than
most people think; however, no matter how great a
parent we are, we can always be better. We all need
help. Let's face it, effective parenting is a lifetime experience.

I have four children and I love them very much.
I'm not the best father in the world, but by God's
grace and with His guidance, I'm giving it the best
shot I know how. No training was provided for me
on how to be a parent, and I have my strengths and
my weaknesses. I may not be what I ought to be as
a parent, but one thing I'm thankful for is that I'm
not what I used to be, nor am I what I'm going to
be with God's help and my family's patience.

As I read and reread this manuscript I was deeply
motivated to work on my weak areas, strengthen my
strong areas and be the father my children need.
Perhaps you will be motivated the same way.

2

"Does Anyone Else Feel Like I Do?"

*"Sometimes I think no one is experiencing
the same feelings of need that I have
for love, acceptance and closeness."*

---❤---

Although they may have a hard time admitting it
to their parents, teenagers have a need to feel that
they belong, that they are loved and accepted. Some
of them feel this need deeply and desperately. Here
is how a few of them expressed it.

I wish that my parents could be more caring, because sometimes when I'm upset they don't act like
they care — they think it's just no big thing. But
sometimes I'm really hurting inside and I can't count
on them to care for me.

♡ ♡ ♡

In school, teenagers feel the need to be accepted,
to become part of a larger group. Often, pressure
is applied to drink, experiment with drugs, or have
sex. Nowhere is this pressure more apparent than
in a one-on-one relationship between a girl and a
boy. A girl wants to be liked and appreciated for
her femininity, and when a boy she likes or even

loves persuades her that only by surrendering sexually can she prove her affection, she will often give
in to the emotional pressures.

♡ ♡ ♡

During junior high I found myself being much
different from my classmates because they all had
boyfriends and were having sex with them. I longed
to be liked by them, so I felt that I must do the
same. At sixteen years of age, while working I found
myself attracted to a man named Dan. He was fifteen
years older. On our first and last date we went to
a little cafe to eat. While we were there we just
talked. As the night progressed, I found myself in
the woods nearby making love to him. After having
sex, I felt like freedom had just been won, and now
I had become just like my friends. I was wrong.
Even though I did what they did, I still felt less
accepted.

♡ ♡ ♡

One primary reason for premarital sex has got to
be insecurity. People all over the globe suffer from
a poor self-image; they long to be accepted and liked
by those who interact with them. Sex provides some
with a sense of security and a feeling of acceptance,
and gives them the assurance that they are liked
and wanted.

♡ ♡ ♡

Going back in my mind to the Friday night I first
gave myself away, I'm trying to grasp hold of a few
of the many feelings, pressures and emotions that
were racing through my mind. We got to a certain

point and the "yes" that came from my mouth over-
powered the "no" that was silently pounding in my
head. I was feeling excitement at the thought of be-
longing to someone and finally being worldly mature
in the eyes of my friends. Afterwards I remember
trying to feel guilty and ashamed for what I had
done, but those feelings wouldn't surface until
months later. For then I was content to be loved
and to be a real part of the crowd.

♡ ♡ ♡

Parents need to realize that children learn about
love and acceptance from them. If parents would
only be the examples that they should be, then
maybe less girls would wind up dead in some hos-
pital, or pregnant and alone, or in some abortion
clinic with a tremendous amount of guilt and fear.
And maybe, just maybe, if parents would tell their
children that they love them, and be affectionate
toward them, then they'd know how to love other
people and be able to make the right decisions about
sex.

♡ ♡ ♡

3

Sex Drives

"Would you be shocked at my private world?
My sex drive can be intense
and I fantasize about sex more than you know."

❤

There is a healthiness in thinking about sex in a wholesome way, a reverent way. It's when the thought life becomes distorted that there is a danger. The problems arise when your sexual thoughts control you instead of you controlling the thoughts.

One of the major causes of divorce is sex incompatibility. Part of the incompatibility is a sexual dysfunction. Often this is caused by sexual fantasizing. When you create in your mind the ideal sexual mate, you're building a straw person who neither you nor your partner will be able to be.

One reason guys don't wait is, a lot of the time they cannot stop themselves; we get to a point where there's nothing we can do to stop ourselves. A lot of the time girls don't know what they are doing to a guy by hugging him and being real nice or sitting in his lap and moving around. The guy might be "just a friend" but all guys have hormones and after

25

girls get those activated there's not much we can do except go home frustrated and angry.

♡ ♡ ♡

I wish that my parents understood I am a sexual being. Even though I am not married or even seriously involved with anyone right now, I still have sexual urges. My parents have difficulty understanding this because they believe that those kind of emotions should only come with commitment. Although I believe that these urges should not be indulged in until marriage, I can't help it when they come upon me. Try as I may, they seem to creep into my mind and body when they will. I wish my parents understood that I do hold the same convictions that they do about having sex before marriage and that I am trying to control my sexual thoughts and urges, but it isn't easy, and I need support to keep from giving in to them.

♡ ♡ ♡

With no clear concept of right and wrong, with my desire to love and to be loved, and with my growing sexual drive, my decision to involve myself in premarital sex was easily made. Unfortunately, I was unable to obtain the love that I had sought, and with so many others also seeking, it was a quick walk from one bed to another. Better luck next time.

♡ ♡ ♡

As teenagers, we are still developing and we're in a very precarious period in our lives. During these years our minds are developing as well as our bodies and we seem to be "stuck" in between childhood and adulthood. We, more than adults, desire to be accepted by our peers. We desire friends and are beginning to be attracted to the opposite sex during this time. Our sexual feelings are very strong, and there have been times when I feel like a "hormone with feet." You might laugh at that but I'm serious when I say that a teen's emerging sexual desires are very strong, and without a fully mature mind to control that teen, peer pressure can be a very loud voice.

♡ ♡ ♡

I believe some of the reasons that people in my age group become sexually active before marriage are an incredible sexual urge during the age of puberty, pressure from society and friends, and the curiosity of wondering what it's like to have sexual intercourse.

♡ ♡ ♡

Sometimes when I sit at lunch with a bunch of other girls we just watch the guys go by, and girls say, "Oh man, I want his body."

♡ ♡ ♡

All of us realize that our bodies change a great deal during the time of puberty, not only physically but also emotionally. We change in the way we feel toward the opposite sex. For some the feeling is just a liking and admiring of the opposite sex. For most there is a strong feeling of desire toward a person, especially if that person is a boy/girl friend. This is one reason people our age become sexually active, to fulfill that strong desire.

♡ ♡ ♡

My college classes have indirectly shown me the
ways I'm maturing sexually, but I wish you and I
could talk about it. Even if I did not date very often
in high school, how could I ever have known what
kind of feelings that kissing can arouse in a young
man and woman? I wish you had told me . . . or
warned me about the desires that grow stronger the
more involved you become with someone. It is
frightening because I want to explain what is happening to me now to my own daughter but I do not
know how I can tell her. Was it different, Mom,
when you were twenty?

♡ ♡ ♡

I have a fear of what my future husband will think
of me. I would want to tell him of my sexual experiences. When I do remember the situations, I thank
God that I was able to say "no" and I am still a
virgin, but I think of how close I was and how hard
it was to say "no." Passion is tough to fight.

♡ ♡ ♡

4

Peer Pressure

"It isn't easy to say no to peer pressure."

♥

The source of a teen's security is usually found in his acceptance by others — especially his peers. The affirmation of one's self-worth, humanly speaking, is rooted in the opinions of others.

When there is an overriding need for affirmation, a teen becomes vulnerable to peer pressure. If a teen senses his or her own uniqueness, it is easier to stand up against the pressure.

We all need positive affirmation. When that encouragement is lacking at home, church or school, a person becomes more responsive to his peers.

Everywhere I looked I was now seeing all the magazines with their ads telling me of the sexual nature of their products, television with their ads and all those sit-coms with their innuendos of sexual prowess. It was everywhere. My friends always seemed to be talking about last weekend at the party, or were always asking me about my experiences. Yes, I had a girl friend. No, I didn't do stuff like that! Yeah, we held hands walking home from school a couple of times. Yes, I liked her. No, I didn't have to prove anything to her.

"VIRGIN." It was worse than having herpes. With herpes my friends would be sympathetic and caring. But "virgin" drew snickers as I would pass in the hallways. No more "What'cha doin' Friday night?" because they knew.

♡ ♡ ♡

Peer pressure. These two small words sum up one of the greatest reasons sex is so popular today. Among guys, a guy is thought of as "cool" or "a man" when he has sex for the first time. He becomes "cooler" and is looked upon with more admiration when he does it repeatedly with different girls.

♡ ♡ ♡

Someone can be tempted to do things as in sex. You can be around a group of people and everyone is pushing you to go ahead and say yes, and you get all of this temptation in you and then you are very confused. You may still be a virgin and hang around with people who are not. They might try to influence you to do the wrong thing by saying, "Oh, you're not cool!" or, "Hear what other people are saying," or, "Look at that guy, he is really going for you."

♡ ♡ ♡

A boy in my school brags that he is cooler than the rest of us because he has experienced sex already. Because of that, a lot of kids went out and tried sex, but they weren't pleased, especially the kid whose parents owned the house because they all got caught!

♡ ♡ ♡

Another reason that comes under peer pressure is the fear of being labeled "inexperienced." To some people, that's the worst name you could call them because it implies childishness. Also, our culture has gotten to the point where a male's reputation is actually strengthened when he is considered "experienced." So, peer pressure is a good reason people in my age group don't wait.

♥

Some teenagers frankly admitted their fear of rejection if they would not participate in sex.

I did a lot of drugs the first couple of years in high school, and in my senior year I started to get away from it because I saw that it was a social crutch. And apart from the drug group there was the jock group, the clean guys. They didn't do drugs, but they had sex, which was their social crutch.

I started hanging around with them and I felt a lot of pressure to make it with women. I couldn't stand the rejection I got from the drug group and I couldn't risk rejection from the jocks, so I gave in. I think everybody needs a support group and I just switched crutches.

♡ ♡ ♡

A lot of my friends tell me about how their boyfriends want them to do sexually active things. When a girl's boyfriend asks her to do sexual things, she's afraid to say no. She thinks by saying no her boyfriend will not want to continue their relationship.

♡ ♡ ♡

In my school, if you're a guy and a virgin, you are nowhere. If you aren't participating in anything and everything you can get involved in as far as vices go, you are a freak. I know that sounds strong, but that's the way my school is. And when people think you're weird, they shy away from you.

———————————————— ♥ ————————————————

Kids, especially girls, feel a lot of confusion and frustration over the unfairness of no-win situations and double standards. This is where strong convictions, stemming from their value system and their sense of their own identity and worth, help teens take a stand.

This is becoming a greater problem today because our culture continually makes it harder and harder for teens to live according to God's principles.

———————————————————————————————————

Society is basically two-faced. If you don't go all the way before marriage, you are a chicken or a goody-goody, but if you get pregnant outside of marriage, you are "loose" or a "slut."

♡ ♡ ♡

A girl's situation is kind of different from a boy's. For instance, if a girl sleeps with a guy before they're married, she is a slut, but if she doesn't she's considered a prude. You could say it's like a double-edged sword — either way you lose.

♡ ♡ ♡

When a new girl comes to our school, other girls come up and ask her if she's a virgin. And if she doesn't say anything, they start saying, "You are! You are!" So even if you are a virgin, you have to lie. I mean, everyone wants friends, right?

So then people know you put out, and guys know in advance that they can get what they want on a date. You can't win.

♡ ♡ ♡

Society has long advocated a double standard regarding sex. Women who lost their virginity prior to wedlock were said to have lost their honor. For men, well, they just gained experience.

♡ ♡ ♡

A girl that does it is a slut, and a guy that does it is a jock, a stud. One guy I know, talking about his ex-girl friend, said, "This slut I went out with. . ."

———————————— ♥ ————————————

The pressure to conform is so great that some teens even will be untruthful about their experiences just to be accepted by their peers.

Some guys lie, saying they went out last night with a girl and did this and that, when all along they didn't do anything with her. They're trying to fit in, because if you don't do it, you're not cool. You're a nerd.

♡ ♡ ♡

I went out with a girl once and we didn't do anything physically, but by Monday morning everyone "knew" we had done all of these things. She was the one telling stories!

———————————— ♥ ————————————

It is important for teens to think through their own dating standards, and parents can help them develop their value systems. The parents' view of life, people, self-worth, the dignity of man, God, and the purpose of sex will play a vital role in determining a teen's sexual involvement.

When a person becomes a Christian, many of the above issues are more clearly focused, and this greatly affects that person's behavior.

Since becoming a Christian I have not been involved in any premarital sexual activity. I have had several long relationships, but the pressure from the girls has almost always been too much and eventually destroyed the relationship. I suppose I might be considered a prude, but I feel that any kind of involvement beyond conventional kissing and hugging is "going too far."

♡ ♡ ♡

5

Pressure Lines

"Pressure lines hit me when I'm vulnerable."

--------------------------♥--------------------------

Never underestimate the heat of the moment. I learned this years ago after time and again seeing strong, dedicated Christians fall to premarital sex. I have heard so many times how convictions that seemed immovable and irrefutable in the light became fuzzy, irrelevant platitudes in the dark.

Any number of factors can come into play to weaken an unmarried person's moral stand: intense emotional feelings, fatigue, outside influences (having just seen a movie with sex in it, etc.), fear of losing the other by not giving in, and so on, but an important element that is often overlooked is "pressure lines."

Pressure lines are those phrases used at a time of vulnerability to manipulate another into having sex. They may seem harmless enough when seen on paper but, used at the right time, they are powerful tools of destruction.

Pressure lines are the "Saturday Night Specials" of relationships, and like the handguns of the same name, these weapons are cheap and inaccurate, and are used only at times of aggressive attack. And they are usually used to render a victim defenseless, even one who is normally prepared for such attacks.

Another common reason [for giving in to sex] is that peer pressure drags the person under. That person is told by the partner that "one time will never hurt," or, "If you love me, you'll want to." This puts the other partner in a very awkward situation.

♡ ♡ ♡

Kids involved in premarital sex say they love each other. In reality, they are really lusting after each other. This is a subtle way to make the act seem "all right."

---------------------- ♥ ----------------------

These are examples of the pressure lines teens use on other teens to influence them, to get them involved in premarital sex.

1. You would if you loved me.
Time went on and he still pressured me. He told me that if I loved him, I would show him. I finally gave in to his threats. After we had sex, we could not go back to holding hands.

2. I want to make love to you.

3. Everyone is doing it.
We think everyone else is doing it so we have to do it to be considered popular. For girls this is a problem because they don't want to be considered "a virgin" all of their lives. This seems to be sort of disgraceful and not very right. When the guys hear

everyone has done it, they sort of feel left out and they do it just to experience it and to be considered part of the "in" group.

4. Just try it once. If you don't like it, we won't do it again.

5. I won't get you pregnant.
I won't get you pregnant if that's what you're worried about. There are lots of forms of birth control to prevent pregnancy.

6. Let me prove how much I care for you.

7. Since we're going to be married anyway, it's OK.
How could I have been so stupid, Laura? Donald talked me into going all the way by giving me such lines as, "We'll be getting married soon. What difference does it make if it's on paper or not? We'll be married in the sight of God and that's all that really matters."

8. If you turn me on, you have to follow through.

9. Sex is no big deal.

10. What are you afraid of?

11. You don't want to graduate from high school and still be a virgin, do you?
Or people (peers) will make fun of your virtue and make you sound as though you have a "hang-up" about sex. When you get to a certain age and you are still a "virgin," people tend to make you feel that you should be ashamed.

12. If it feels good, do it.
Sex is fun if we don't let our Puritan heritage interfere and make us feel guilty.

13. Sex is a natural thing to do.
Sex is just another appetite like being hungry or thirsty, so why not satisfy it? Why all the fuss?

14. Sex is a private affair. What we do in private is nobody's business.

15. Well, why not? Are you gay or something?
If a guy doesn't fornicate, he is usually teased a lot, mostly about his sexuality. He is called "homo" (homosexual), "fag," or even "chicken." This can really get on a guy's nerves after a while and actually force him to have sex just to get the rest of the guys off his back — just to get them to respect him.

16. But you know I'll still respect you in the morning.

17. Don't be a baby about it.

18. If we only go so far and not all the way, it's OK.

19. Look at so-and-so. They're doing it and they are Christians.

20. If you won't have sex with me, I'll find someone else who will.

21. You won't catch anything.

22. There's something wrong with you if you don't.

The general idea of sex today is if we don't "do it," then something must be wrong with us. In other words, everyone is participating in sex, so it's OK for us to "do it" also. By sticking to older values from past generations, we risk ridicule and rejection. The general attitude seems to be that society knows more about our needs than God does.

23. That's so old-fashioned.

24. You don't know what you're missing.

25. I want to do it now so I'm prepared for marriage.
I felt people not married should not play around with sex because it wasn't ours to play around with because we don't always desire the consequences. His next response to me was, "I have sex so I will know what I'm doing when I get married."

The following are examples of how teenagers justify sex in their own minds, the pressure lines they use on themselves.

1. Kissing turns me on, and it's not enough.
I don't want to have sex all the time; it's just that kissing turns me on and it's not enough.

2. It's OK to test her out. If you buy a car, you test-drive it. I want to be sure she's the right one.
I used to say all the time to my Christian friends, "But you must try on the shoe before you buy it."

3. I don't want to lose my boyfriend.
"It was different for me," Debbie countered. "My

boyfriend was the only one I ever had sex with. I loved him. I needed him. I wanted to keep him."

4. It makes my boyfriend happy . . . it pleases him.

The girl wishes to do almost anything to make the guy happy, and it really hurts him emotionally not to have sex because he loves her, and/or physically if he has a high sex drive; then the loving girl friend may feel so guilty and obligated when seeing her boyfriend's hurt that she may give up her former standards.

5. If I do not get it on with this person, I will become frustrated. I need to.

6. I feel like I'm "supposed" to.

7. I want to be accepted by my peers.

If the people you want to be around are involved in premarital sex, they will put pressure on you to act or at least think the same way. Peer pressure is especially hard on guys. If a guy has sex, it is usually viewed as a conquest, and it makes him more popular among the other guys. On the other hand, a guy who hasn't had sex or doesn't want to is often viewed as a wimp or a geek or something. It's not the ones who have sex that have a bad reputation but the ones who don't have sex.

8. He paid for the date so I feel like I owe it to him.

Many teenagers, while dating, will feel that the other person expects it of them, and he or she might expect it. They feel an obligation, of a sort, to that person to have sex with them, especially if the other person has spent a lot of money on them.

9. All I want is some companionship.

10. No guy is going to ever wait for you if you
    don't give him what he wants (sex).
Some boys who knew my standards joked about
it. And one of my friends even told me, "Hey, no
guy is gonna wait around for you if you don't give
him what he wants (sex)."

11. It would be boring being married and having
    sex with only one person.

6

Influence Of The Media

"TV, movies, and radio all tell us it's the thing to do."

---❤---

The media, especially television, is one of the most powerful influences on young people's moral actions. The media pressure for sexual involvement is overwhelming. Research shows that the average teenager sees 9,230 acts of sex or innuendos encouraging sexual involvement a year. By the time a person reaches twenty, he has seen more than 92,000 acts or alleged acts of sex in his brief lifetime.

The problem is that no one on TV ever seems to pay the price of illicit or "casual" sex. For example, when was the last time that you, the viewer, saw someone on TV get a sexually transmitted disease? You are probably like the overwhelming majority of people — you never have. The impression given is that it never happens.

That impression is fiction! It's a lie! Today 33,000 Americans will contract a sexually transmitted disease. That's twelve million this year!

Sex on TV and in the movies is glamorized as the sure cure for all relational ills and as the ultimate joy of life. Our young people find it extremely difficult to combat TV.

Here's what teenagers have to say about the pressure of the media.

The pressure from the media to engage in permarital sex is so intense, Mom and Dad. I am sure you are aware of some of it at least. Contemporary music is the worst; I bet that nineteen out of every twenty songs are about sex or infatuation. Even with a Christian world and life view, I cannot listen to the radio without thinking about what it will be like to be married and have sexual relations with my husband. Those same thoughts become visualized in 90 percent of the movies today that could be described as "decent." Those mental images terrify me because I cannot be an immoral Christian. The two do not coincide.

♡ ♡ ♡

Sex screams from the billboards. Cigarette ads show kids lolling in the grass. The hi-fi stereo ads show kids on the floor. The suntan lotion ads show kids on the sand. Everybody is lying down with someone.

♡ ♡ ♡

People are not being told the truth about premarital sex...I wasn't. What we are being told (mostly by the media, but also through our peers) is that premarital sex is OK. . . . We're told on TV shows, commercials, magazines and cartoons (great for kids) that this is the lifestyle of those around us. Unfortunately, we are not being told about the other side of the coin.

♡ ♡ ♡

Society also had much to teach me: Test-drive that car before you buy; a free sample just for you; no-risk offer; a ten-day free home trial; money-back guarantee if not totally satisfied. I was learning that commitments need not be made on faith alone, and I could always return the unused portion.

One more thing about peer pressure. If you really want to see how strong it is, just tune in to any secular rock station on the radio or look at the record jackets in a store. Turn on the TV to some of those soap operas many of the girls in my school see, or go to one of the movies that is aimed specifically at teens. Then tell me if the promiscuous lifestyle, homosexuality, rebellion and anti-Christianity is spread through the mass media. Then consider this: This is what today's teens are tuned into 365 days out of the year. It's very hard for teens to resist peer pressure and it's sad to see many Christians sucked into its grip.

♡ ♡ ♡

The things teenagers watch and read make them pick up wrong attitudes about sex. Like soap operas, they make sex look all right. You're always cheering for the right person to sleep with the right person. Sex without marriage is simply accepted behavior. You always root for the good person, no matter what they are doing.

♡ ♡ ♡

One night we went on a date to see the movie, "10," stopped on the way home at a bar where he bought me a couple of drinks (I was not drunk, though), and finally on the way home we took a detour and had sexual intercourse in the back seat of his mother's car. I wish that, if the television channel is going to show how much fun the act is the night it happens, they would also show the extreme guilt that is felt the next morning. Of course they cannot show that; it may hurt their ratings. I really wonder sometimes if the broadcasting company realizes how much of an impact the television has on the "younger audience."

♥

The following extended excerpt from an essay allows us to get inside the mind, heart and emotions of a teen struggling with his or her culture. We're able to see the intensity of the conflict between a spiritually sensitive adolescent and the sensual pressure caused by music and the media.

"You're the object of my desire . . . Light my fire . . . Emotions are so strong . . . Please make love to me . . ."

Caught in an unguarded moment, I find myself unconsciously listening to another song that blatantly encourages premarital sex. "Oh, great, not this song," I tell myself. Disgusted, I scan the radio for another station, in hopes of finding a Christian song being played.

Hey, God, are You there? It's me. Can we talk? Sex is such a dominant influence in my life; I can't run away from it. How can I not be influenced by radio and other sources to jump into bed with my girl friend? How can I handle it?

Everywhere I go, there seems to be some thing, some song, or some person to tell me that it's OK to have premarital sex. For instance, let's take the movies. You know how the majority of today's movies are aimed at me, the All-American Teenager. Almost every single picture I've seen has had some inclinations toward sex. The teenage boys in the movies appear to have only one motive: to go to bed with a girl. TV is no exception. I would think that the public viewing of TV would place some restrictions on sexual innuendo. And they do. Somewhat. Quite similarly, most of the ads on TV, radio, and magazines use sex to sell their products. I certainly have to admit that a beautiful woman catches my eye, no matter what the product may be.

At school, sex may be part of a lunchtime conversation. Of course, dirty jokes are prevalent. I have to admit that some of those jokes are kind of funny, and I can't help but laugh myself. So You see, the presence of premarital sex is always around. Sometimes it's very subtle and I barely realize that it's there; other times it's so strong that I really have to struggle in order not to give in. The presence is always there, on TV, radio, at the movies, and at school. Always.

Pornography is an important issue too. Though porno doesn't even come close to being as popular with girls as it is with boys, it affects us all in a way. Maybe because sex in pornographic magazines and films doesn't contain a one-man-one-woman act anymore. Actually it contains one man and two women, or maybe two men and one woman, or maybe several of both. How do I know? Because I'm just like any other teenage boy. Pornography is no rough task to get ahold of. Most store owners don't care how old you are. The same applies to video shop proprietors, who couldn't care less if you're eighteen or not.

If You stop to think about it, You realize how many lives become affected by television. Many marriages end up on the rocks due to the fact that television depicts having an affair as being not so serious a matter. They show teenagers having sexual intercourse and they do not experience the consequences, guilt or hurt that could occur after such an extremely serious act takes place. Sex was designed to be something carried out by a married couple, but they are making it out to be something that teenagers should experiment with.

When viewers look at how television affects premarital sex and teens, they could pretty much end up putting the music industry in the same category. That is, teens can be highly influenced by the way music affects them. I mean when one hears songs like "Like a Virgin," "Flesh for Fantasy," "Just a Gigolo," etc., and when teens see "rock stars" as being role models, they try to pattern their lives after them.

♥ ♥ ♥

7

Sex Education

*"Sex education gives us
the how-to's, not the how-not-to's."*

----------------------------♥----------------------------

What the first two students say here provides a revealing introduction to the whole topic of sex education.

As society changes and medical technology advances it is becoming increasingly harder to say no when the temptation for premarital sex arises. The reasons that worked for my parents and grandparents have gradually been eliminated.

♡ ♡ ♡

Many schools have instituted sex education programs. The information they give out does clear up misunderstandings the students might have had, but they also unintentionally encourage experimentation. The kids have all the correct information, and all that remains for them to do is test it out.

♡ ♡ ♡

In a sense, public schools promote premarital sex. In Alabama a student in a public school is required to take one semester of Health before he is allowed to graduate. One portion of the Health class that has to be taught is sex education. This course is taught on a co-educational basis; that is, the boys and girls in the same class. No one wants to ask questions with someone from the opposite sex sitting next to them. Some teachers will allow you to take the course independently if you choose; however, if a student chooses to do this, he is greatly teased and ridiculed. Therefore, most students end up taking this class. No moral values are taught in this class, only the facts about sex and birth control.

♥ ♥ ♥

If a kid decides to have sex, there are many options: birth control pills, abortion, adoption, and more. And guess who gives these kids these options? Their parents and "sex education teachers." If there were no way to assure kids that they would not get pregnant, I'll bet not as many of them would mess around with sex.

The problem is they educate us on how to get around having a baby, not that we should not have sex.

I was sitting in one sex education class and the nurse said, "There is only one sure way to keep from getting pregnant and that is not to have sex, but that isn't very practical." As far as I am concerned that is very practical since she was speaking to freshmen and sophomore high school students.

♥ ♥ ♥

The schools almost say that it is all right to have sex by giving health classes that tell you all the ways of having sex without getting into trouble.

♡ ♡ ♡

One contributing factor to teenagers and young adults getting involved in sexual immorality before marriage is curiosity. All their lives they have been told that it is wrong to be involved before marriage. Consequently they seek in innocent ways to find out more about it, talking to friends, then reading pornography, seeing movies and filling their minds with these things to the point where their minds are obsessed with it. As Christian teenagers grow up at home, they are told it's wrong . . . and that's it. They need to be told more than that, why it's wrong and how to use the Word of God to fight these temptations. Most teenagers are just told at home and in school to read the Bible, obey your parents and elders and do what's right.

❤

"But we need sex education. . ."

The media saturation in our culture demands that our young people be told about sex at an early age. The ideal situation is for sex knowledge and feelings to be communicated in the context of the home. The home is the best atmosphere to discuss not only the mechanics or biological aspects of sex, but also its moral, ethical and spiritual dimensions.

The fear of sex education in the schools, as voiced by so many essays, is based on the fact that their hands are tied when it comes to teaching a positive morality covering the ethical and spiritual side of sex.

Dr. Edgar S. Woody, M.D., in an editorial in the Journal of the Medical Association of Georgia, writes about the public school sex education dilemma:

> The philosophies upon which some of these [sex education] programs are based state that they cannot make value judgments regarding the rightness or wrongness of sexual activity. I disagree. I submit that unless they do, and until they do, they will be hurting the people they are most trying to help. Teenagers do not need help managing sexual intercourse nearly as much as they need help in forming their own moral codes.
>
> With the situation as it now is, teens get little if any reinforcement to abstain from sex. Let us not blame the times or society, the while sidestepping our personal responsibility in setting guidelines for the sexual behavior of our children. We must take a stand even though it may be unpopular and not in line with the times. I shudder to think what succeeding generations will be like if we do not do this. If we fail to teach our young people a set of values, what are they going to teach their children?[1]

The magnitude of the public school sex education dilemma is seen in the heartbreaking teenage pregnancy rate. This year there will be 1.1 million teen pregnancies and nearly 50 percent of these pregnancies will end in abortion. The rapid transmission of sexually transmitted diseases represents another area in which there is a desperate need for sensitive, thorough sex information.

Adolescence is a time period in one's life of intense feeling and confusion. It is during this period that teenagers grope for any information about sex available to them. Unfortunately, most of the readily available information is pornographic in nature or advocates "safe sex" with contraceptives. There is not much readily available and visible information I have seen which would serve to guide a young adult in the right direction. Even in many good Christian homes talk of any facet of sexuality is frowned upon. We then turn to other means of sexual education such as street talk where only a partial, distorted truth about sex is given. Even when the topic is addressed by my church youth group, the discussion never gets to the point which needs to be addressed the most: What does the Lord want for me?

♡ ♡ ♡

So many times today you see a teen that gets caught up in premarital sex because of the impact his parents have on him. What I mean by that is that oftentimes parents do not take the time to just sit down and talk with their teen about such matters. So many times, the child ends up having to venture out on his own because he hasn't really been taught the consequences. Then too often when the parents do talk with the child, they speak in a harsh tone saying, "YOU'D BETTER NOT!!!" thus leading the teen to get involved in premarital sex as an act of rebellion.

Contemporary churches are spending less time teaching their young people that having sexual intercourse before marriage is sin, and parents feel like they have lost contact with their teenagers and, therefore, give up on the idea of trying to teach their children about sex. So how are these kids forming their beliefs about sex? By doing it. And after experiencing such a "great" thing, how could it be wrong? So they have developed a false belief.

Some reasons for the need of sex education are parents' failure to explain the subject to their children. Because of parents' embarrassment in talking about sex, or not spending enough time to adequately discuss the subject, often young people do not learn the facts concerning premarital sex. Many parents want their children to learn these facts in their sex education classes in school. But as articles in magazines such as *Time* and *Newsweek* state, some school systems do not provide sex education because parents are against the teaching of sex education in school. They believe that sex education should be taught in the privacy of the home. But my parents didn't do it there.

Many parents have the same attitudes concerning sex as my teachers in elementary school did. Describing sex is very awkward and embarrassing for them. Consequently parents will often invent answers to probing questions asked by curious children. The most widely used answer is probably, "The stork brings babies." I think that's wrong because it's a form of lying, and it can cause confusion in later years. The friend I mentioned earlier was told by her mom that kissing causes pregnancy. Because she had been told this when she was a youngster, as a sophomore in high school she still didn't know the truth concerning sex.

♡ ♡ ♡

Virginity and the sacredness of sex is something all teenagers should be informed of. My Christian high school does not offer sex education classes and feels it is the responsibility of parents to inform the children. What if parents fail to take on this responsibility? Teenagers are curious, and their ignorance, due to lack of adult responsibility, might get them mixed up in a premarital sex situation. The teenager is responsible for his or her actions, but is it entirely the fault of the teenagers since they were not informed of the dangers of premarital sex? It is not. Partial responsibility must be laid on those who neglected to inform the teenagers.

The only things kids know are what they learn in locker rooms and school halls. Parents won't teach their children about sex at home, so they learn the hard way — at school and on the streets. In their hearts, teenagers who engage in premarital sex usually blame their parents. To an extent it is the parents' fault because of the failure to open up to their children on the subject of sex. Instead, parents turn them off and change the subject. When parents turn away from the subject it makes them all the more curious to learn about it — even on their own.

♡ ♡ ♡

A poll of 1,000 teenagers revealed that sex information was gained in the following ways:

(A) Only 32 percent of the girls and 15 percent of the boys were informed about sex by their parents.

(B) 53 percent of the boys and 42 percent of the girls found out from friends their own age.

(C) 15 percent pieced together the information they had received from other sources.

(D) 56 percent of these young people acquired their sex knowledge between the sixth and ninth grades and 18 percent learned about sex before the fifth grade.

(E) A full 88 percent of these young people felt they needed more information about sex than they had received from their parents.

♡ ♡ ♡

One problem that seems virtually inevitable is the feeling teens get that something like this couldn't possibly happen to them. Maybe it won't, but who can guarantee that? Proper sex education by the parents can help the child make the correct decision when considering premarital sex. While this is a good idea, some parents become embarrassed at the thought of discussing sex with their children. This usually leads to buying a book for the child which usually gets thrown in the closet and is never heard from again. All of this new knowledge can also have a somewhat negative influence on the child. Suddenly there is an urge to try out this knowledge.

♡ ♡ ♡

8

"Grow Up!"

"Suddenly everyone tells me to 'grow up!' "

---------------------------- ♥ ----------------------------

Few people realize what they are saying when they tell young people to "grow up." Do they mean "act like an adult" in the fullest sense? No. Parents who admonish their teens to grow up do not mean, "From this point on, you are to assume all of the rights and responsibilities of contributing adult members of our society." They don't expect their kids to strike out on their own, get married, buy a house, invest in mutual funds, join the PTA, or do any of a thousand other grown-up things.

Grow up, in fact, means, "Be like an adult in some ways but not in others." This is the message we want to get across, but it sometimes backfires. Teens look around for a model to see what grown-ups are like and they see, at nearly every turn, grown-ups going to bed with each other. The sexually oriented adult society leads the young people to this thought: *Aha. Sex is an automatic part of being grown up. The most mature thing I can do is have sex.*

This was a new concept to me. I had never associated teenage sexual involvement with a need to act mature until the abundant references to it appeared in the essays. I have to admit, it jarred me.

In addition to our general adult society, many parents also individually put pressure on their young person, and don't realize they are doing it. When a parent tells a young person to mature, 99 percent of the time they do not take the time to explain what they see a mature person as being. So the young person turns to his peers' definition of mature, in other words, engaging in sex. Teens today need parents who will explain the differences between maturity and having sexual relationships.

Sometimes I think a lot of teenagers become sexually involved because of their poor relationship with their parents. If their parents pressure them with a lot of responsibility, they feel as if they can take all the stress away with a sexual relationship.

♡ ♡ ♡

I think that too many parents are pressuring their kids to grow up too fast. Then they leave them alone and don't teach them that sex before marriage is sin.

———————————————— ♥ ————————————————

One problem parents face is the double message being heard. On the one hand is the message that comes to teens through television and music. "Go for the gusto." It is OK for adults to be involved in nonmarital sex. It's all a part of maturity, being a man, being a liberated woman. The admonishment is, "Grow up . . . act more mature. . ." But on the other hand, in many homes and at church, they are told not be sexually active.

The signals are mixed. We parents need to help our confused teens find that balance of being a kid living in an adult world. Let's not hurry our children to "maturity."

SECTION II
"How You Can Guide Me Through My World"

9

What Your Teens
Say They Need From You

*"I learned about sex from the street.
Believe me, this is not a good place to learn it."*

———————————————— ♥ ————————————————

"It says in this book," said the young man to his friend, "that teenage boys think about sex 17 seconds out of every minute."

"Really?" replied his friend. "That's unbelievable!"

"Why?" asked the first.

"Well," said the friend, "what is there to think about the rest of the time?"

Teenagers in a nutshell, right? Maybe.

A *TeenAge* magazine poll of teenagers in 59 countries showed that the topic of sex is of primary concern to American youth. "304 out of the 305 teenage respondents in the U.S. cited premarital relations as one of the three most important issues facing today's youth. By contrast, just 29 percent of those in other countries said they considered premarital sex a major problem — the lowest ranking of any of the six topics listed in the question."[1]

Even though it may seem that sexuality is the overriding issue in the lives of many teenagers, it is actually only one facet of their lives. But just as garlic, only one ingredient, can submerge all the other flavors in a complex recipe, so can one part of a teenager's life drown out all the rest.

Teenagers are people in transition. They are neither children who need constant supervision nor adults who are ready to take on the full responsibilities of life. They are somewhere in the middle.

But in the midst of physical changes, social pressures and growing independence, they remain above all, people. And just as with people of any age group, *all aspects of their lives are interrelated,* so that an experience in one area may greatly affect another area.

This is why, when I asked teenagers to give me messages (especially about sex and relationships) that they wanted passed on to their parents, they said, "Mom and Dad, please show love to each other . . . please talk to me . . . please accept me even when I fail . . .make me feel important . . . please make Christ the center of our home life . . . don't lock me in a cage, but please don't think I can handle everything alone — I may not say it, but I need you."

They didn't want books on the facts of life. They didn't demand unlimited freedom to live their own lives. As you will see in their own words, they asked that the bonds of love, affection and communication in the home be the foundation for their lives, their refuge in a world of overwhelming internal and external pressure.

Regardless of how well you know your teenagers, you can never know with certainty what they are thinking. You may not see how one event influences other events, such as a fight with a boyfriend affecting a girl's athletic performance. You may only see the result of these two events (i.e., a poor athletic showing) and never know the cause.

Teenagers are very aware of how seemingly unrelated experiences in their lives work together. Unfortunately, many parents don't see the correlations.

What happens in conversation around the dinner table could have a direct bearing on what happens in the car when your teenager is on a date. Is your son groping for love and not finding it at home? Does your daughter assume, since her father never shows love for her mother, that men can only express affection through sexual advances? And if she were to become pregnant, would anyone believe that her parents' relationship was a major contributing factor to her predicament?

To better understand how relationships in the home can affect dating relationships, we need to realize that all of us long for intimacy, even though we may not be aware of it or recognize it as a motive for many of our actions.

God has built into the life of each person a desire for intimacy with others. In fact, the so-called Sexual Revolution was actually a revolution in the way we try to achieve intimacy. There was nothing revolutionary about sleeping around — people have always done that. The big change was in the way we began to perceive relationships. We were willing to settle for something cheap and empty, albeit very intimate in one way, rather than bother building long-term relationships that were intimate on several levels: emotional, spiritual, intellectual, social, etc.

A relationship between a man and a woman should build intimacy on all levels, culminating in physical intimacy after a lifelong commitment to each other has been publicly declared. But the Great American Vending Machine promises quickie intimacy that avoids the incumbrance of commitment. Teenagers, bombarded by messages of happiness in relationships through sex, may not want to bother looking for real intimacy. Worse yet, they may not believe it is possible.

A child learns about relationships at home. A study reported in *Psychology Today* asked high school girls to evaluate their relationships with their mothers, including the amount of affection shared, how authoritarian the mothers were and what kind of role model the mothers were. Each girl was also asked to evaluate her relationship with her best friend.

The researchers found that "when teens feel close to their mothers, they also have warm relationships with their friends. . . . Friendships formed, in part, to compensate for a lack of love at home, in contrast, don't seem to make a satisfactory substitute. 'Deviations from the ideal in the mother/daughter relationship make it difficult for girls to develop close friendships,' [researcher] Yanof says. They have not had 'the opportunity to develop the adequate levels of interpersonal trust and personal autonomy that . . . are prerequisite to the capacity for intimacy.' "[2]

But a girl's diminished ability to be intimate with others doesn't diminish her longing for intimacy. It is a part of her nature to desire intimacy. And when she finds that she can neither be intimate with her mother nor her friends, where will she turn? There's a good chance she will turn to boys to find the happiness in relationships she wants.

Unfortunately, she may well buy the message on the movie screen that tells her every Friday night, "Sex makes relationships great."

And perhaps the saddest part of all is that outside sources, such as movies, are today's sex education instructors, even for Christian kids. As one young man wrote in addressing his parents, "You may not know it, but I learned about sex from the street. Believe me, this is not a good place to learn it."

Another one wrote, "Mom and Dad, it was your responsibility to tell me about sex before I discovered it the wrong way. You did not fulfill your responsibility which was given to you by God. You're supposed to lead me in the right path."

10
Parents' Relationships

"Parents, please show your love for each other by your words and actions."

———————————— ♥ ————————————

As we saw in the first chapter, teenagers, like people of all ages, are looking for love. God has made us with a longing to be loved and wanted, and when that longing is not filled at home, people are forced to turn elsewhere. And when a model of love is not shown at home, it becomes hard for teens to distinguish love from lust or manipulation, and that leaves them open to sexual involvement, the most tangible form of affection they can find.

I was not surprised to hear teens say that much of their understanding of their own sexuality comes from observing their parents' relationship. When children see in their home a marriage based on love and respect, they know that lifelong relationships are possible: They have seen one work. By watching displays of affection that back up affectionate words, children learn how relationships can be built on more than self-gratification.

Children take what parents tell them about relationships, filter it through their observations of their parents' marriage, measure this against what they hear from other sources and develop their own view of how relationships work. This view is then played out when these children reach the age where relationships with the opposite sex become important to them.

Mom and Dad — Thanks for staying together through "thick and thin." Things were so tough so often. Too many others have quit when things get rough, but you two taught me what real love is about — commitment! Thank you both.

♡ ♡ ♡

Thanks for instilling in me a healthy self-image by loving each other and loving me so much. I've never doubted your love for each other or for me, which has really helped me to love other people and look forward to marriage. Thank you for keeping your love fresh and working at it every day. Through watching your marriage all these years I have seen the reality of God's love.

♡ ♡ ♡

To both my parents — Thank you for loving each other and sticking through the tough times together. Thank you for giving me a Christian home. You really love each other and have always had fun together, and I thank you that I really belong to a family.

♡ ♡ ♡

Dad — thanks for staying with us through the hell that our home has been, with Mom's illnesses and depression and our rebellion. I have never known anyone like you.

♡ ♡ ♡

I feel so blessed by God that He made you my parents. You have been the two best role models in parenting, in marriage and most of all in Christianity. May I be able to pass on what you have taught me.

♡ ♡ ♡

Thank you for continuing to love each other. That makes me feel so good you wouldn't believe it!

♡ ♡ ♡

Thank you that your love for each other has set such an excellent example for my brothers and me in our future relationships.

♡ ♡ ♡

I especially appreciate my dad's love for my mom (and us kids) — it makes me realize that God must really be a great Father!

───────────────── ♥ ─────────────────

These young people recognize the need of godly, caring, loving parents whom they can pattern their own lives after. The love of a father for one's mother is a priceless treasure. Jesus established the basis and need for healthy parental models or examples when He said in Luke 6:40, "A pupil [child] is not above his teacher [parent]; but everyone, after he has been fully trained [raised], will be like his teacher [parent]" (NASB).

We had our problems like every other family in the world, but we sensed a love from our parents that wouldn't fade with the future.

They demonstrated a unique blend of masculinity and femininity which complemented each other well. Individually, they carried out their roles, sometimes feebly, as is characteristic of the flesh, but there were more occasions where that magnetic attraction that brought them together became a wonderful display of permanence that cemented their hearts and our home.

♡ ♡ ♡

My parents are unique; they're still happily married after 22 years together. Hard to believe today, isn't it? They've raised five children, who are only six years apart from the oldest to the youngest. Believe me, we didn't make it easy on them. Through long nights, dirty diapers, jobless times, moving across the country, fires and floods, they've stayed together and been faithful. They aren't perfect, and it hasn't been easy; but that's what true love is all about.

♥

The above comments can be very encouraging and motivating to a parent. At the same time we need to acknowledge the negative response to parental modeling.

You guys have been a real example of love to us, but what about each other? Dad, please don't ever tell me again that if it wasn't for my brother and me, you would leave. I HATE that! And Mom, please lose weight so you look like yourself again. Please, you guys, stay together forever!

♡ ♡ ♡

Dad — I forgive you for leaving Mom, and I realize in your own way you love me and my brothers. I hope and pray you find the peace you have always searched for.

Mom — you are more like Christ than anyone I have ever known. You have such unconditional love for Dad and us kids, and I will always believe you were the only mom I could have made it through life with.

♡ ♡ ♡

Daddy, I wish you would have been more sensitive of the women you lived with: a wife and two daughters. You rarely showed emotion or affectionate love, and as a result your daughters have had a difficult time learning to show love. You are insensitive to Mother's needs, yet she loves you *so* much. She needs to feel special in your eyes.

♡ ♡ ♡

Mom and Dad — I know that you have been having severe marital difficulties for the last year. I want you to know that your marriage is very important to me, even at my age (31). If your marriage fails, it will be as if the world's values have won out, as if there is no way marriage can last for anyone. My children have so many friends from broken homes, and they look at my marriage (which is a good one) as an extremely important thing. They need the assurance from you also that marriage is not dead.

♡ ♡ ♡

Dad — In the 10 years since the divorce the love and respect I had for you has turned more and more into hate and anger. I used to defend you and your actions but I don't any more.

♡ ♡ ♡

I wish they knew how much I wanted them to love each other.

♡ ♡ ♡

I have never been especially close to my parents, and they are not Christians. They don't even seem to be close to each other anymore. In fact, sometimes I don't even think they like each other. I try to imagine them as a young couple in love, and my mind draws a blank. I so desperately want them to feel love.

♡ ♡ ♡

Mom, I don't understand why you let Dad push you around when you argue. You love each other, but you fight like you're senseless.

———————————— ♥ ————————————

Are you wondering what kind of views about sexuality and relationships your children are developing by watching your marriage? Will they enter a relationship having learned to look out only for their own interests and desires, or will they be like the young woman who wrote, "I hope that when I get married my husband and I will have the love for each other and the love for Christ you two have"?

It is my desire to see more parents modeling a love for each other that will flow over to their kids. A positive role model of parents in love gives tremendous security to a child.

11

"Love Me"

"Mom, Dad, I need to know you love and accept me."

♥

Kids want attention, and sex can be the "pressure point" they use to turn parents' heads to get that attention and love.

Our kids are saying, "I want to be loved and accepted totally apart from what I do." The fear of having to perform to be accepted dominates the thought life of most teens. All of us are driven to be accepted and loved. When we discover a conditionless love and acceptance with our parents, we are set free from trying to earn a dominating, emotionally draining, performance-based love.

Sometimes I really don't try my hardest in school; but when I do try, they don't see it and don't comment. I want them to accept me for who I am. I know they want what is best for me according to God's will, but they (Dad especially) *always* want me different. I'm never right about anything.

♡ ♡ ♡

I wish my parents could know that I want to really measure up to their standards, but *every day* I feel I've failed, which is why I treat them so coldly. I am ashamed of myself and I don't want them to get too close to see where I hurt. It seems I'm always trying to be competitive with my sister, but I have given up on myself.

♡ ♡ ♡

Dad, I love you for who you are as a person. You don't have to buy my love with your monthly checks. It comes to a point where I feel like I owe you something back because I know you expect me to respond with some appreciation of your financial support. But I feel like you aren't proud of me unless I do something outstanding in your eyes [age 21].

♡ ♡ ♡

I fell into the trap of looking for love in sex because my need for love was not being met by my family. I took what I could get. But strangely enough, after I was pregnant, my family was very supportive and helpful, even through the adoption process. This was a real blessing.

♡ ♡ ♡

Teenagers are just like everyone else. They have many needs, desires and fears. They need to feel loved and to express love. If their homes and families don't provide the love and attention they crave, they always seem to find someone who will. They need someone to make them feel accepted and secure. In many cases families today are falling far short of meeting these basic needs of their young people.

The concepts of proper affection, caring, and communication all need to be demonstrated in today's homes, both in actions and in words. This is where teenagers should begin to learn what true love is really about.

♡ ♡ ♡

Everyone desires to be needed and to feel loved, and many young people believe that through premarital sex they will receive love. Fathers and mothers are often first striving to meet the financial obligations of the home, and thus their lives are tied first into a place of employment. Money has captured the hearts of Americans, and yet money hardly purchases enough to meet the wants of families and most importantly, money does not purchase the love for which young people yearn. In addition, with the abundance of divorce papers being signed, young people often wonder if they have been divorced from a parent's love.

♡ ♡ ♡

I am someone who really doesn't talk to my parents that much (especially my dad). What I would really like to say is that I love them a lot. Even though I may not show it, I do love them. Also, I wish my mom would say she loves me more often than she does. I know she loves me, but I think it's something every kid wants to hear often.

♡ ♡ ♡

I would like to know why you never say that you are proud of me. I try my hardest to please you but you never say anything.

♡ ♡ ♡

I thank you for loving me and showing your affection for me daily. I appreciate so much your concern for my life and your acceptance of my decisions and choices. I'm especially thankful that you give me freedom to make choices, let me fail, and then still express your love to me.

♡ ♡ ♡

Mom and Dad — I needed you to tell me that I was unique, that I was special. I needed to be given the tools to live as an adult in an adult world. You didn't help me to develop a sufficient ego to make it in this world. I can't rejoice in *who I am* any more. I wish you wouldn't have made me cling to you like you did. I wish you could have let me go so I could grow up.

I needed my parents to tell me that I was *okay*. You did everything for me and it was the worst thing you could have done. Now nobody respects me any more. Most importantly, I don't respect myself. I have to learn to forgive you, but I am so scarred from the past. I have a hard time really believing that Jesus loves and cares for me because I was always made to feel unworthy of anything. I have no security in my life.

Why did you reject me so much?

♡ ♡ ♡

I did not know that you approved of me until I was 23 years old. Then you said you were proud of me. Why did it take you so long? Your acceptance could have saved me a lot of heartache that I am still going through at age 39.

♡ ♡ ♡

I want my parents to realize how crucial their positive, uplifting and encouraging remarks are to me, especially since they pertain to *who I am,* not just *what I do.* As a single adult, I still derive the greatest and most substantial awareness of my self-worth from my parents, more than any other people in the world.

♡ ♡ ♡

I wish my parents knew how much I really love them and appreciate what they have done for me, but I also wish they knew how I suffered as a teenager from the love, inspiration and understanding I felt I never received.

♡ ♡ ♡

Thank you for loving me and spending time with me as I was growing up. You gave me everything I ever wanted: your love and your time.

♡ ♡ ♡

Mom — I love you, and I admire you for your strength and commitment to Dad in the midst of his selfishness. You have truly taught me so much from your life.

Dad — I forgive you. I want you to be happy so that you can have joy in your life. Please love me and show me that I am OK. Your acceptance is so important to me.

♡ ♡ ♡

My parents are jerks sometimes. My dad is —
about 89 percent of the time — but I guess they are
everything I can expect them to be. I want them to
know that even though my IQ is not 150 I am still
worth something. I want to talk to them, but since
we don't like a lot of the same things they pass
judgment on me and think I'm weird. I hate that!
I'm not very close to them because my dad can't
accept me the way I am.

♥ ♥ ♥

I LOVE YOU. These three words were never used
in our home and because of this I have suffered.
Until a few months ago I was afraid that nobody
would ever love me, or worse, that I might not ever
be able to love anyone. But I have discovered that
Jesus loves me so much that He died on the cross
for me. I know that there is hope.

I can now freely say that I love you and mean it
from the heart. I hope that you find Jesus, too.

♥ ♥ ♥

I wish they knew that I try my best to please
them, but I'm a kid and I'm supposed to mess up.
And I thank them for recognizing this. I love them
very much and I thank them for loving each other
so much.

♥ ♥ ♥

I'd like to know why they think I'm such a loser,
why they don't think my graduation or things I'm
doing are important enough to make time for. What
have I done that is so terrible that they won't even

tell me they care about me? Most of all, I want them to know I love them. I really mean that.

♡ ♡ ♡

Mom and Dad, I realize we don't get along too well. I'm not sure why, but the more we try the worse it gets. I know you love me. I just sometimes wonder if I'm wanted. I mean, you have asked me to leave. I guess in a year or so it won't really matter because I'll be gone. Oh well, I love you. Thanks for all the trouble.

♡ ♡ ♡

I love you, and I know you love me. We've expressed it many times. I don't understand why you must put me down, Dad, to feel like you are the father.

♡ ♡ ♡

My dad never hugs me. I'll hug him before I leave for school, but he sort of stands there. I love my dad, but he actually gives me a funny look when I hug him. And I tell him I love him, and he just mumbles something. I guess it's hard for him to show love because of how he was brought up — macho.

♡ ♡ ♡

I had an abortion today. I had an abortion and I have been sick, physically sick, ever since. But the vomiting and the cramps cannot compare with how I feel mentally and emotionally at this moment.

I know that abortion is wrong. So you wonder why I did it? Because I was stuck, that's why. I got myself into a situation that I saw no other way out of. How did I get myself into this situation? I don't really know. I think it started when I was little, really little.

We went to church every time the doors were open, and sometimes when they weren't. I had (and still have) good, godly parents, and they wanted and expected me to be the same way. I think it really hit home when I was about six. I had done something wrong, I don't even remember what it was, but I told my mother about it. After I had poured out my soul to her, she just sat there and looked at me like she was really hurt and said, "Honey, we expect better than this from you. Mommy and Daddy want their little girl to be good. I'm so disappointed in you!"

Although I was only six, I can still feel those words ringing in my ears, and I decided right then that if I ever had a problem or did something wrong, I would not tell my parents. I couldn't risk having them be disappointed in me.

♥

The above is a good example of the fact that when one's acceptance is based upon performance, and then performance is poor, the person has to hide it out of fear of rejection. The risk of disappointing a parent will cause a child to put up a defense mechanism to keep the parents from really knowing him or her. This leads to isolation, and to seeking intimacy and acceptance from someone else.

12

"Listen To Me"

*"Just talk to me . . . Listen to me . . .
Try to understand me."*

---❤---

When you listen to someone, you are saying to that person, "You are important. What you have to say is important." It communicates to a child, and the child realizes, "I'm important."

About seven or eight months after Dottie and I were married, she came to me rather hesitantly. I could tell she was hurting. "I don't think you love me," she confessed.

"What?" I exclaimed. "You've got to be kidding! I love you more than anyone else on the face of this earth."

"Honey," she replied, "I really don't think you are interested in some of the areas of my life that interest me. I don't think you care about some of the 'little' areas."

Ooh! That was like driving a knife through my heart. Immediately I asserted, "But I do, too!"

I was amazed as Dottie explained why she felt that way. "You never listen to me. I will start to share something with you and you will cut me off or change the subject. Or I will start to share something with you and your mind is off somewhere else. You often pretend you're listening, but your mind is on a free-speech platform in Bolivia." That's my wife's way of saying, "Darling, you're thinking about something else while I'm talking to you." (I got my start doing free-speech debates with Marxists in Latin America.)

You know what I discovered was happening? Because I had never learned to listen to people, I was unintentionally communicating to my wife that I didn't care. She was starting to retreat into a shell.

"Attention to what our mate says," writes Richard Austin, "is one measure of our respect. Too often we hear the words of a conversation but do not really hear the message. Listening to words and hearing the message are quite different."[1]

Since I had not made a concerted effort (and sometimes no effort at all) to listen to Dottie, I was communicating to her that what she had to say wasn't important to me. What a way to strangle a partner's enthusiasm!

Listening is one of the most profound ways to show someone that you take them seriously, that you care, that you value their opinion. Dr. David Augsburger puts it this way, "An open ear is the only believable sign of an open heart."[2] Here's how Augsburger relates effective listening to a person's self-esteem:

"If you listen to me, then I must be worth hearing.

"If you ignore me, I must be a bore.

"If you approve of my views or values, then I have something of worth to offer.

"If you disapprove of my comment or contribution, then I apparently had nothing to say.

"If I cannot be with you without using your comments for self-evaluation, then leveling will be impossible. If I am preoccupied with what you think of me, then I have already shut you out."[3]

I have a very caring father who always listens to my problems. I think parents should take the time out to listen to their children because that child could really be hurting and having problems. By parents talking and listening to their children about what the Bible has to say about premarital sex, premarital sex can be avoided.

♡ ♡ ♡

I wish they would listen to me more and try to understand me.

♡ ♡ ♡

Dad, why did you never listen to me? Why did you never encourage me?

♡ ♡ ♡

Mom and Dad — I wish for once you would really listen to me. Pay some attention to me and treat me with respect. Give me the chances that you have deprived me of just because my older brother and sister screwed up. Treat me as my own person. I wish you would show your love for me, if you have any, or at least be friends with me. Dad, I wish you would quit treating me so awful and finding fault with everything I do. Quit putting me down and calling me names. I love you.

♡ ♡ ♡

I wish my parents knew how much it hurts not to be listened to and how degrading it is never to be given their complete attention. Please forgive me. . .

♡ ♡ ♡

A teenager's search for identity is enough reason for parents to have understanding, but in addition to this, parents must understand the contemporary elements that teenagers are exposed to: threats of nuclear war, sexual proliferation and other glamorously expressed interventions of a Christian person's fulfillment.

Also, I believe that it would be easier on teenagers for adults to realize that teens are relatively immature to life's experiences. This, combined with the instinct to discover, brings about a sense of curiosity, anxiety and awareness toward the opposite sex. A teenager's search for security leads to a tendency to conform to society, a desire to attain worth and fulfillment through the use of sex. Society's message of "the more the better" almost makes teenage sexuality a sport, a game of manipulation.

♡ ♡ ♡

I would like my parents to know that I am not as good as they think I am.

♡ ♡ ♡

I wish my parents could understand what it is like being a teen in the eighties. I wish they would accept the fact that times have changed. My friends and I are not simply content to get married after we graduate from high school, and the guys I admire aren't looking toward a future of working in their parent's business, and having a kid before they're twenty. NO, we are children of the eat-and-go generation. I have grown up with a purpose in life. My friends and I are looking toward four to ten years of college and then starting successful businesses, always looking for increasing satisfaction in life. Sex has become a part of young adults in the eighties, because it enhances a certain aspect of life. It is seen only as another pleasure in life on the road to total happiness.

♡ ♡ ♡

The pressures I feel in engaging in premarital sex outweigh the consequences. I feel that I need to experience what others are in order to keep up in my society. Also, sometimes I feel so alone, and the comfort sex can bring from someone I can relate with satisfies my longing at the time. I sometimes wonder if engaging in sex now will affect me when I'm married, but it seems that in all the marriages I know, sex plays such a small role it won't really matter. I wish my parents could understand and accept me and my generation and the way we are and that I could share all this with them and they'd agree.

♡ ♡ ♡

I would like to *talk* to my dad. He's too busy for me, and when we do talk, he doesn't listen or try to understand me.

♡ ♡ ♡

I wish my parents could understand me as I am so I wouldn't always have to pretend I have it all together.

♡ ♡ ♡

I wish my mom knew about some of the stuff I've done behind her back, like telling her I'm doing one thing then doing another. I also wish she knew about some of the stuff I've done in dating relationships.

———————————— ♥ ————————————

When you have a living father or mother who is indifferent to you, you always have the hope that maybe someday they will hear you. But when you have an indifferent parent who dies, then you've lost all hope. Loss of hope often leads to depression. It can easily turn to anger. That child can interpret death as the parent further deserting him or her. The following is an example of bitterness resulting from a feeling of desertion.

Dad, I wish I understood why you never did what a father should do while you were alive. You never respected me, talked to me in depth, taught me to be mature, guided me as I was growing up. You didn't trust me or believe I was sincere. Why didn't you love Mom? Why did you marry her if you didn't love her? Why didn't you want to spend time with me? All I wanted was your attention, love and time.

♡ ♡ ♡

13

"Trust Me"

"I need to know you trust and believe in me."

---❤---

I would like to see more parents open up to their children and become friends with them. Until kids and parents have mutual trust in their relationships, how can kids be open to share their intimate feelings about the opposite sex or even their outlook on premarital sex?

Trust is a key ingredient to open, honest communication between any two people, but even more so between parent and child.

I wish they would have more trust in me and know that I would never lie to them and that I love them.

♡ ♡ ♡

Dad — I resent the fact that you did not see me the way I was. I also resented your wanting me to be like my cousin instead of letting me be myself. Why didn't you trust me to do the right things? You were constantly on me. You never affirmed my worth. You were too negative toward me.

Mom — You were the one who should have made a difference. You didn't. You allowed the bad to get worse. You were too weak to protect your own children from a father who treated them badly. Things could have been better for me if you would have countered him.

♡ ♡ ♡

I want my parents to trust me and the decisions I make with my friends, etc. I wish they *knew me* well enough to have the trust to know I would do the right thing.

♡ ♡ ♡

Dad — don't give me everything. I need to work and even struggle for things.

♡ ♡ ♡

My parents sometimes think that every girl is after my body. Every new girl brings a lecture on my standards of conduct and morals. I'm 18 years old — if I haven't learned about sex and life by now, then it's too late. What I mean is, I'm past the stage where repetitive lectures do any good. I've heard it for years in various forms, so if you can't trust me on a date now, then give it up. Experience is the only teacher left to me.

Fortunately, I agree with my dad's view. He and any girl or her parents have nothing to worry about as far as I'm concerned. But the way they talk, you'd think they saw a lurking Don Juan in me.

I'm all for instruction, but after you've taught a child, you've got to trust them because either they listen and obey, or they'll flaunt instruction and no amount of repeating will do any good.

We all know temptation is hard, but I've got to fight my own battles with God's help. Mom and Dad can't do it for me. That's life.

♡ ♡ ♡

I wish my parents would trust me and understand that I am trying my hardest.

———————————— ♥ ————————————

Over and over again teens wrote that they wanted to be brought into the family problems. If children are kept in the dark, their imaginations can get out of hand and blow the problem completely out of proportion. Many times the teen is aware of family or marital problems before their mom or dad ever acknowledges or discusses them. There needs to be wisdom on the parents' part as to how much to discuss with their kids.

Mom, you're going through your second divorce and I know you have a lot on your mind. I really wish you would talk to me about your problems and not just keep it inside.

———————————— ♥ ————————————

One frustration teenagers feel is expressed in these statements:

There are 50 things I want to say to my parents: Let me grow up! (Repeat 49 times.)

♡ ♡ ♡

They can't hold me down like a baby and protect me forever. I need to learn to take care of myself.

♡ ♡ ♡

I wish my parents knew that I don't want to be insubordinate but sometimes it happens. I feel the amount of leniency and freedom is sufficient, so I don't require more. I just need time to discover my life and I wish they would support me in it.

♡ ♡ ♡

I would like for them to have more faith in me and treat me like an almost-adult. I wish they would trust me more and I wish they would respect me.

♡ ♡ ♡

Trust — parents need to trust because sooner or later they won't have a choice in the matter.

♡ ♡ ♡

I want my dad to appreciate my feelings and attitudes about things. I want him to know I care about him but that I need to be myself. He needs to accept my opinions and decisions and trust me.

♡ ♡ ♡

I want my parents to know I should be able to choose which church I want to go to. I have been raised in a church where I never learned anything about the Lord, and now that I have found a church where I do, I should be allowed to go there.

♡ ♡ ♡

Parents and rebellion also play a role in premarital sex. If a parent accuses a child of something he has not done, he feels as if he might as well do what he has been blamed for. It also mentally hurts him that trust in him has been betrayed by his parents for a reason that does not even exist.

♡ ♡ ♡

I would like my parents to understand that I am getting older and need to be able to accept more responsibility than I am given. The real world is a difficult place, and I am going to have to be able to face it. My parents are very good to me and give me lots of guidance, but I need to be able to do more things on my own — with their understanding.

♡ ♡ ♡

I will struggle, but I can make some decisions on my own now. Just give me a chance. I know you want the best for me all the time, but give me a chance.

♡ ♡ ♡

The act of sex loses sanctity to be replaced by a feeling of victory, as each time a teen has sex, he "earns" a trophy to be proudly displayed before his peers as self-significance. I believe that the parents should be looked upon from more of a "caring, friendship" standpoint. A "parent friend" to impose

no need for secrecy, but rather an available "knowl-
edge-caring" outlet with a small will to advise and
a strong will to listen.

♡ ♡ ♡

14

Teens Turn To Others
For Acceptance

*"Nobody else ever shows love for me in any way
so I'm doing whatever it takes."*

---❤---

The absence of parent-child communication says
to children, "Nobody is listening to you." Then there
appear the boyfriends or girl friends who are more
apt to listen to them than their fathers or mothers.
That's when they begin to find their basic love and
acceptance from their peers.

Our culture says, "If you love me, you will have
sex with me." The teens constantly wrote about their
confusion regarding the difference between love and
sex. The desire to be heard goes into the need to be
loved, which leads to sexual involvement as an expression of that need.

If parents can detect this need their child feels
for love, maybe they can help so their child won't turn
to a girl friend or boyfriend to try to find love through
premarital sex.

If teens can realize they can feel good about themselves without engaging in sex, a lot of the teenage
pregnancies will be banished and teens won't have

to turn to their "mate" for premarital sex. They can just say no.

♡ ♡ ♡

Diane was an average 16-year-old. She went to school and had a part-time job, and she had a boyfriend. She also had parents who loved her. They had trouble showing it. And though they did, she never saw it or realized it. So she turned to her boyfriend and started having sex to find love and security. Some young people today feel the need to become sexually active, to feel accepted and wanted. But what really motivates them?

Maybe it's to get back at their parents because they feel left out or ignored and want their parents to hurt also because they know their parents would be hurt if they found out they were sleeping with someone.

♡ ♡ ♡

The other major reason for engaging in sex is teenagers feel the need to be loved. This is expressed a lot in the way a young child feels love from a mother. If that mother holds the child, cuddles the child and shows affection for the child, then the child knows his mother loves him. That is how a lot of teenagers feel. If someone shows affection for them by having sex, they then feel that person must love them or at least care for them. This of course is not always true, and sometimes that person ends up getting really hurt.

♡ ♡ ♡

The search for a constant love causes young people
to turn to sex. Not feeling loved by their family,
they explore new avenues to satisfy their needs.
Feeling worthless and neglected causes young people
to treat themselves and their bodies the same way.

♡ ♡ ♡

Another reason, which is rarely expressed but
often happens, is family problems. They feel unwanted by family members, but when they engage
in sex they feel wanted and a part of someone. A
death in the family often brings someone so down
that they need to have the feeling of love that goes
along with sexual activity. They need this sense of
security.

♡ ♡ ♡

Some people feel neglected by parents and family
so they turn to the wrong places for what they think
is love and have sex to feel wanted and needed.

♡ ♡ ♡

They tend to reach for any kind of affection that
they see, just to take the place of the lack of love
they have experienced. This brings to mind a young
girl I know who has a problem relating to guys
without becoming sexually involved. She has a typ-
ical family environment but it lacks one thing — a
father's love.

♡ ♡ ♡

As most people grow up they are rarely built up
and significantly put down causing intense feelings

of insecurity and low self-esteem. Whenever someone is encouraged and complimented, he develops a liking for whomever has done this. People have learned how to play on each other's emotions and they will say anything the other wants to hear in order to get the things they want. In my high school youth group I had a good friend named Keri. She had little feeling of self-worth and when Dennis came into her life he made her feel worthwhile. She knew he was an immoral person, had a child already, and had just gotten out of jail, yet she stayed with him because he made her feel good. Keri quit attending church and when I talked to her a few months later she told me she and Dennis were very physically involved. She said, "I know it is wrong but nobody else ever shows love for me in any way and so I am doing whatever it takes to keep Dennis from leaving me." It ripped my heart to see that the world is so cold that many people have to turn to things they don't believe in to feel any personal value.

♡ ♡ ♡

The next place people go to find love is in a relationship. A boy-girl relationship provides a feeling of security and love that often is not to be had elsewhere. It is within this relationship, a person wanting so badly to be accepted, that sexual relationships begin. Many times teenagers are not even aware that they are searching for love, and yet they want to be loved by someone so much that they will do anything the other one wants them to do for the security of the relationship.

Once a sexual relationship starts, it becomes habitual. Every time the two go out or see each other it is just expected that sexual activity will be a part of it.

♡ ♡ ♡

Affection is embarrassing to some parents so they "prove" their love by spending money on their kids and not showing affection and love. But these days a teenager needs love, security and most of all, affection. And when there is no love in the home they will look for it everywhere else.

♡ ♡ ♡

Your parents are just too tired to realize that you are down and you are left with no one. Does this need of yours just go away? No, I'm afraid it doesn't. The next day you are at school and the first thing your boyfriend notices is that you have something bothering you. He comforts you, talks to you about your problem and you feel 100 percent better. *Wow!* you think, *from now on I will go to him with my problems and forget about bothering my parents.* You get more involved and closer to your boyfriend as each day goes by. In this situation one thing leads to another and you end up getting yourself in a vulnerable situation. The parents could have prevented this event from taking place.

♡ ♡ ♡

And many teens often turn to sexual involvement as a means of escape. In today's society many homes lack love and affection from parents. Too many parents are caught up in the whirlwind of our busy world and don't take the time to care about what is going on in their child's life. If a child can't find love and affection at home, he or she will inevitably seek for it elsewhere.

♥

The following heartbreaking story underscores the need for us parents to develop a loving, caring, trusting relationship with our children. This begins through open, honest conversation where each one's feelings can be shared.

Fearfully dreading the realization, Carolyn cries quietly in her dark and lonely room. She must tell Mark, her boyfriend of three months, and her parents, that she is pregnant. Carolyn is only sixteen.

Carolyn's parents always saw her as a wonderful child, but never gave her much of their time or attention. I feel this is a major reason many teens have premarital sex and get pregnant. Many parents think if they provide their kids with the worldly things, the kids won't need their love and time. But they do, and when their parents don't give it to them, they go to boyfriends or girl friends for it.

I think parents and teenagers need to communicate more. They need to open up and share more. In Carolyn's situation, this could have kept her from this unwanted pregnancy.

♡ ♡ ♡

15

Parents' Divorce

*"I feel your divorce is my fault
and you don't really care about me."*

♥

One of the greatest sources of a teen's insecurity and guilt today is the fear that "my parents will get a divorce." It creates insecurity in the sense that "I'm not that important to my mom and dad." The teens blame themselves for their parents' problems. Whatever tension has developed between the parents in regard to the children, the kids see it as their fault and tremendous guilt develops. The emotional effect for the teens can be, "Nobody loves me. I'm not worthy of being loved."

The result is sexual involvement that has a double message for the parents: (1) I want attention; and (2) I want you to know I am worthy of being loved.

Another reason for the premarital sexual activity of teenagers is a feeling of insecurity. Whether this emotion is formed as a result of rejection by one's peers or an unstable home life, the feeling causes the young person to reach out desperately, grasping for answers. Teenagers generally have low opinions of themselves; therefore, the need for affection and love is even greater in this age category. This insecurity is due in part, I feel, to the increasing rate of divorce in the American culture. The teenager growing up in a broken home has not experienced the benefit of seeing a successful relationship between his parents. The teenager, in turn, grows unsure of his romantic relationship, and is willing to do whatever he feels necessary to maintain it.

To take an example of premarital sex — two months ago the headlines of a national UK newspaper heralded that a sixteen-year-old boy was now to be the father of three children, and this phenomenon all stemmed from the fact that his parents had divorced and his sense of insecurity and boredom had led him to seek his own sexual relationship.

♡ ♡ ♡

I think one of the leading causes of sex among teenagers today is when their parents get divorced. I have gone through it and I know how they feel. I felt that my parents did not care for me. I felt left out and rejected. The Bible says in 1 Peter 5:7 to cast all your care upon God and then He will care for us. I blamed God and could not understand why He made the divorce happen to me. Later I realized that through the divorce God wanted to show me how to be more mature and He wanted me to realize that when you do not marry the one that He has for you, then most of the time the marriage does not work. I think that teenagers, when they go through their parents' getting a divorce, are hurt and very emotional. Then when a boyfriend shows that he cares, they feel that the only one they have to turn to is him.

♡ ♡ ♡

Because of this high divorce rate, children raised now don't have a stable environment in which to live. There are 12 million children of single parents and every year one million teenagers run away from their homes. Looking at their parents, young people have no concept at all of permanence in a family and they cannot know the true meaning of "the two shall become one." (This explains why a man leaves his father and mother and is joined to his wife in such a way that the two become one person, Genesis 2:24.)

♡ ♡ ♡

In today's society, where the number of one-parent families is increasing, young people can easily become isolated. It is more than likely that the single parent goes out to work during the day, leaving the child alone for long periods of time. The child therefore feels insecure and sometimes unloved, and he or she may try to find this security and love in a relationship with a member of the opposite sex.

♡ ♡ ♡

Of course, there are more causes for these breakdowns of values on premarital sex. The broken homes of divorced parents encourage teenagers to find intimate love and attention through others to replace what is missing at home. Two working parents make privacy readily available for teens who need or want to fill this gap. I wish parents could experience our sexual and peer pressures. They would know how hard it is to make difficult decisions and understand our vital needs for love and acceptance.

♡ ♡ ♡

Because of the divorce rate and lack of respect for marriage, teenagers have begun to forget that sex is a communication and commitment of love that helps two individuals express their special, personal relationship with each other. I mentioned earlier two words which I believe go hand in hand: life and love. I believe that these are both gifts from Christ.

The divorce rate in the U.S. has grown a lot over the past few years, and its effect upon young people has been great also. Everyone knows that the world is in disorder, but when a young person also has to come home to disorder, the general feeling becomes, Who can be trusted? and, Where can this trust be found?

♡ ♡ ♡

Jessica's mother had a boyfriend and was divorcing her father. When Jessica's mother tried to use her authority, Jessica ignored her, reasoning that her mother had done many things much worse than she had ever done. As a result, Jessica lost all respect for her mother.

She was a strong girl and had always managed to overcome the pressures of sex. Her emotional turmoil was great, and she gave in thinking she would try sex once. After all, didn't her mom do the same thing? Sex became an outlet for the pressures at home.

♡ ♡ ♡

Family problems often contribute to premarital sex. Divorces often make it hard on the child or children of the family. The feeling of being loved seems to disappear or may never have been there in the first place. A person may feel that if they find someone to love, they will have the love they want and need. This often leads to premarital sex.

♡ ♡ ♡

Divorce rates have gone higher than ever, giving more children single parents. Single parents should not be looked down upon if they are being "parents," but a lot of single parents are plain "singles." These single parents are dangerous to their children, because while they are single, they re-live their youth by dating, and no longer hold up their authority by disciplining their children. They get so caught up in dating that their children become a problem. Who can have a romantic night out with the kids? The children are left at home more and more, and eventually are ignored. If the child protests because he wants attention, the parent turns against him and accuses him of "being rebellious, always siding against me whatever I do." The poor child feels unloved and threatened, and if this child is a teen, he seeks love and is conned into thinking he can get it with sex. Peer pressure is a disaster the world faces every day. It's a part of life and reality.

♥

Because a child seldom understands the situation when a divorce takes place in his family, he automatically assumes it is his fault somehow, and he feels guilty. Usually, there is a considerable amount of tension in a family prior to the divorce, but instead of taking ownership of their own actions, the troubled individuals blame a child for some of that tension. The child internalizes the blame, and his guilt is intensified.

The first thing a parent must do to help the child avoid feeling guilty is to communicate what is happening. This is extremely important, even though it may be especially difficult if the marriage has broken up because one or both partners were unable to communicate.

It is also important not to put the child in the middle of the parents' difficulties. Parents need to avoid criticizing or blaming each other in front of the child, and should not force him to choose one parent over the other.

When a teenager reacts to his parents' divorce with denial, the same way some people react to a death in the family, it sets the stage for further guilt. He hangs on to the hope of his parents' reconciliation, refusing to accept the breakup. The parents must communicate the finality of the divorce so the teenager does not have unrealistic hopes that if he can just do something, Mom and Dad will get back together. His guilt increases when he inevitably fails.

Finally, the child may express anger toward one or both parents for breaking up the family, particularly if one parent is involved with another person. It is best for both divorced parents — and for the children — that the parents not get involved with anyone else for at least a year. That lapse of time enables the child to adjust to the changes in the family structure and increases his sense of security, which then helps him steer clear of sexual involvement.

16

Christian Homes

"I need a home life which is consistently centered around biblical values."

♥

These kids showed tremendous wisdom and insight into the need for spiritual values not only in their homes but also in their own personal lives. It was encouraging to read essay after essay about how important to a teen his or her relationship with Christ was.

In a culture void of absolutes, of what is right or wrong, teens feel the need for a deep spiritual dimension to their lives. They see the parents as the primary source for these values.

I wish my parents knew how much I want to become a stronger Christian! Both my parents are Christians, but we don't talk about it much. We all go to church and we pray and they have taught me well. I just wish we could talk about the Lord more!

♡ ♡ ♡

Dad — I love you and I wish when I was younger we had spent more time together. And although you and Mom are both Christians, I wish you would have been a stronger spiritual influence in my life.

♡ ♡ ♡

Dad, why did you quit after-dinner devotions after only a week just because we complained that we wanted to play instead? We were only little kids!

♡ ♡ ♡

I think parents need to inform kids about what sex is in the beginning, and also should tell them the Scriptures. When you're young it's really confusing, because there are so many things you don't know, and you need to have some backup help like the Bible. But I think sometimes parents don't want to talk about it.

♡ ♡ ♡

Parents may use another approach to the topic of sex by acting like it doesn't exist. This is not a very good idea. In fact, it is probably the worst idea they could think of. If parents expect their children to do the right things, they have to be there to guide them and help them along through the good times and the bad times. They should make sure that they have a strong religious background and knowledge of God and of Jesus. If parents do this for their children, then they can be pretty sure that they will make the right decisions.

♡ ♡ ♡

I wish my parents knew how much it would have meant to me if our home had been more dedicated to the study of God's Word. I wish they would renew their own devotion to each other and to God. I wish my dad would put Christ first in his life. I wish they knew how important these things are to me.

♡ ♡ ♡

Most teenagers aren't properly educated in sexual matters. They know what comes naturally, but they don't understand God's interpretation of sexual love. They don't know they are doing wrong because they haven't been exposed to the right. They have no religious background or else it isn't a firmly sound background. They are ignorant in a highly promoted subject, thus, they tend to make unwise choices.

———————————————♥———————————————

So much of knowledge about sex and sexual behavior comes from sex instruction involving only the biological issues. The lack of a moral context leaves a teen facing some paramount decisions without the proper training to make these decisions intelligently and morally. The choices facing our adolescents today are awesome enough, but the lack of moral direction makes the barrier between the teen and an intelligent and moral choice insurmountable.

Not only is it the responsibility of parents to teach their children about sexuality, but it is also clear in God's Word that they are to instruct their offspring in the ways of God (Proverbs 22:6; Ephesians 6:4). I take this to mean that through our parents we receive our initial character training and development. If proper communication takes place in the

home, a child will grow up with the character necessary to make right decisions. He will be able to
discern what is good and what is not. The combina-
tion, then, of thorough instructions on human sexuality and biblical character development will better
equip the young person to meet sexual temptation
with strength and precision.

♡ ♡ ♡

I'm glad that you have taught me what is right
and wrong and have helped me to have Christian
morals. I love you both.

♡ ♡ ♡

It seems that parents often are as naive about how
behavior arouses physical desires as are their teens.
Parents do not seem to understand their responsibility to prepare and educate their children about the
drives of the opposite sex.

Girls should be taught that men are aroused by
sight. Therefore, the teen girl needs instruction concerning modesty. A father needs to be sure that his
daughter does not leave the house dressed in a
manner that would arouse her date. It seems that
in today's society anything short of nudity is modest.
Parents must refute this philosophy with biblical
instruction on modesty.

Parents should also teach their sons how significant
touching is to a woman. A young man may touch
a girl not realizing the importance of that touch to
her. It is not sufficient to say, "Be careful and don't
go too far." Parents must explain the difference between the sex drives of young men and women.
They must point out what actions and what type of
dress would be sexually arousing. Then the parent

can teach the teen how to be careful and how to avoid circumstances and activities that would result in "going too far."

♡ ♡ ♡

As a Christian, I am glad I have a God that gives me strength. I have been raised against premarital sex, and I thank Mom and Dad for raising me in that way.

♡ ♡ ♡

Thank you. I love you so much for raising me in church and in a Christian home; for allowing me to become a responsible, level-headed young lady with high morals; for stressing the importance of male relationships (sex) and waiting for God's choice mate.

♡ ♡ ♡

Mom and Dad, the three most important persons in my life are God and you because you are the three people who have been my examples and my molds for my life. And without the influence of this sacred triangle I fear to think how I would have turned out. I love you both with all my heart and soul.

♡ ♡ ♡

Mom and Dad, you have been true to what God called you to be. And God has used you to make me a person He can use. Thank you so much!

♡ ♡ ♡

Believe that I appreciate all the wonderful values and examples you have set before me. I appreciate the love you gave me. I am sorry for all the times I have disappointed you or hurt you.

♡ ♡ ♡

Thank you for being godly parents. You have both taught me a lot. I haven't been the best daughter — please forgive me. I feel I have the best parents in the world. You have always given me a lot of support, and I couldn't have made it without you.

♡ ♡ ♡

I wish my parents knew how much I loved them and respected them. They gave me a firm foundation on how to live through Christ and I'm so thankful I know what love is all about.

♡ ♡ ♡

I am so thankful that God gave me you as parents. Thank you for giving me the values and morals that I have and for taking me to church all those years. Thank you for telling me about Jesus and for being an example of Christian parents.

♡ ♡ ♡

17

"We Don't Communicate"

*"I need you to create an environment
in which I can safely share
my experiences, feelings and failures."*

---------------------♥---------------------

Teens show a tremendous need to be able to share feelings, and especially failures, with their parents. They're saying, "Please ask me about my frustration and confusion regarding my sexuality." It is important for a parent to realize that failures in life are part of the overall learning experience. Our culture is so performance based that teens sense an overwhelming fear of failure, believing it will short-circuit the love and acceptance of their parents. A child needs to see and experience God's grace and forgiveness in every area of life — especially in the sexual realm. One of the best ways for our children to learn and see God's grace in action is through us, their parents.

When kids don't feel free to talk to their parents about sex, they rebel as a way of communicating to them their needs.

♡ ♡ ♡

I wish my parents could understand more about my sexuality and the pressures I feel about wanting to engage in sex. I wish I could freely communicate about my feelings and thoughts that intrigue, motivate and sometimes haunt me with guilt.

♡ ♡ ♡

I wish I could talk to you about the things I fail in, not just the things I succeed in. I need you to tell me you care.

♡ ♡ ♡

I wish that over the past few years we had made an attempt to get to know each other as people and friends, not just parents and daughter. But none of us seemed to know how to go about it.

♡ ♡ ♡

I want my dad to know that he is not the only one who has to cope with stress every day. I feel that if we communicated more, we could both relieve a good deal of that stress. Being a male, it is more difficult to say I love you, but you know what? I love you, Dad.

♡ ♡ ♡

I've wanted to tell you how badly I wish I could talk to you about my feelings concerning you, myself, my boyfriends, and the pressure I feel from my friends, but I always felt I couldn't talk to you. I've had to teach myself how to deal with my problems and I have felt very alone. You don't know how many times I have just sat in my room and cried. . .

♡ ♡ ♡

Thank you for your love and concern. I only wish
you had been more vocal in discussing my spiritual
needs. You never probed deep enough to understand
my pain. As a consequence, I have often covered
my true feelings and anxieties.

♡ ♡ ♡

They don't know who I am because they haven't
taken the time to find out.

♡ ♡ ♡

Dad, I wish you would take more interest in me.
We hardly talk because, as always, you are so wrap-
ped up in your own life that you just withdraw
every time I try to get close to you.

♡ ♡ ♡

I don't feel like talking out my problems with my
mom because she is always trying to pry stuff out
of me. I don't appreciate getting "20 Questions" at
the dinner table about my boyfriend, like: "What do
you two talk about? Why don't you plan ahead? Are
you sexually active?" I don't feel like telling her
those things because when she starts in on me I
feel like saying, "It's none of your business."

♡ ♡ ♡

The both of you are great parents; however, I just
wish I could have a better relationship with Dad.
Dad, the reason I talk to Mom more is she always

listens. Every time I try to talk to you, you never listen or you just lecture me and you don't even understand.

♡ ♡ ♡

I love you. I really wish that we could be more intimate and open with one another. If you could listen to me rather than convincing me of your ability, I would feel much more complete. I love you.

♡ ♡ ♡

Although at times I have tried to talk to you, you never hear me. I just wish for once you would hear me. All I ever wanted was a home with lots of love. A home where the family is close. How hard is it to love?

♡ ♡ ♡

Dad, I'd like you to know that, even though I don't act like it sometimes, I really do love you. It just seems that some of the time you want to spend too much time with me. Sometimes I think you're too perfect because it seems you have no flaws. I think it's hard for me to tell you that I have imperfections. But I know you would still love me.

♡ ♡ ♡

I wish I were freer to reveal my innermost doubts and dreams without getting "edited." I can't be as vulnerable as I would like with them because they can't listen to me without imposing their opinions and their own goals for my life on me.

♡ ♡ ♡

Sometimes I know I need someone to talk to and I'd like to talk to my parents because they have been there.

♡ ♡ ♡

I think another important thing is for the parents to let the kids know that it's OK. Parents should let their kids know they are not going to condemn them. You shouldn't be afraid to talk to your parents about it. You shouldn't think your parents are going to hit you over the head or send you away or something.

———————————— ♥ ————————————

The above comments show how much teens want a home filled with love. They long for a place where there is no lack of acceptance and where one can share not only the positive feelings, but also the negative ones without the fear of rejection.

The following reflections by kids will be an encouragement to you as a parent. These kids give us some lofty goals to head for in our families and home environs.

———————————————————————————————

Another reason for not having sex before marriage is it would hurt my mother's feelings. This may not seem important to most people, but it is very important to me.

♡ ♡ ♡

I don't think there is anything I would say to my parents now because it has always been so easy to talk to them.

♡ ♡ ♡

I want my mom to know that I hope to be like her some day. In fact, I'm going to tell her that tonight.

In losing my dad when I was 13, I learned how important it is to tell people things you want them to know *now,* because tomorrow may be too late.

♡ ♡ ♡

I have no message for my parents. They know *everything* about me, my worst and best sides, and have always encouraged the free expression of my thoughts and feelings through their unconditional love.

♡ ♡ ♡

Thanks for the time we spent together, especially during and after dinner when you made us kids tell what had happened in our day while everyone listened. I felt important and learned to communicate better than any of my friends (age 27).

♡ ♡ ♡

I've heard about all the problems with teens getting along with their parents, and not being able to be open with them. But I can talk to my dad about anything. I think that this is possible in most situations.

You see, my dad wasn't a Christian till I was about five, but his moral standards and determination were high.

♡ ♡ ♡

I would like to tell my parents how much I appreciate all that they give me, the support they give me, and though it's sometimes hard to show, I love them. I would just like to open up to them.

♡ ♡ ♡

Thanks for always being there when I need you. You are different from other kids' parents. Thank you for letting me share things with you and you with me.

♡ ♡ ♡

18

"Talk To Me Early"

*"Talk to me early and often,
and tell me what I need to know."*

---------------♥---------------

All three age groups who wrote essays overwhelmingly stated the importance of *parents* sharing about sex at an early age. Many said that by seventh grade it was too late. Many teens wished they had heard it from Mom or Dad earlier. Kids felt they weren't prepared for the moral onslaught.

Also, a number of them commented that many small talks were more effective than "the big one."

Dangers are something that we are warned about constantly when we are young. While my mother warned me countless times of the danger of playing with matches, nobody ever really shared that premarital sex might scar one just as badly as any flame might. Because of the constant warnings about the dangers of fire, I was never burned. I was not as fortunate in the area of premarital sex, as it took years to remove some of the scars it left behind.

♡ ♡ ♡

I wish that I could go back in time with the information I now have, and change everything. I would have been better off if there had been someone there to guide and help me. Certainly I could not talk to my parents about it — they did not even know that I kissed guys back then. I also could not very well bring up the subject with my friends — they were as uninformed as I was at that age. I had nowhere to turn, and I realize today that I turned in the wrong direction.

This is the main reason I am writing this paper. There are many scared, uninformed girls out there, just like I was. I just want to help them. I don't want them to go through what I went through. I felt worthless and empty, and suffered much guilt.

♡ ♡ ♡

How do people get such negative perceptions of sex? One reason is that it is a no-no to discuss. It makes parents uncomfortable when the subject is brought up for discussion, usually because their parents were the exact same way. Due to this discomfort, parents neglect to counsel, warn, and advise about the use or misuse of this important gift from God. Yes! From God! Sex was God's idea first. He planned it. According to Genesis 1:31, we were created excellent in every way. That includes our sexual abilities.

Instead of hearing about these special abilities from parents and other correctly informed authorities, young people hear about sex from their friends and through the media. Magazines, television, billboards, newspapers, and movies are centered much of the time on sex. In one way or the other, everything seems to relate to it. Music pushes it too. According to these sources, sex is OK under any circumstances if that is what you want. The underlying motto is, "If it feels good, do it."

♡ ♡ ♡

Despite the fact that I grew up in the Bible belt, and had many Christian friends, no one ever told me that premarital sex was wrong. Not even my mother. She didn't want to bias me with her opinion, so she never told me one way or the other.

I believe that this is one major reason that people of any age participate in premarital sex. They are never given God's perspective.

♡ ♡ ♡

Mom and Dad, I wish you would have been more open in communicating with us as we were growing up, especially in confronting issues of growing up. You should have talked to me before I got into trouble instead of after.

♡ ♡ ♡

Parents, share God's love and concern with your children. Make sure you let them know He is concerned about their whole lives. Be open in sharing with them that God understands about their sexual feelings. Even with today's supposedly "liberal" sexual attitudes, the parents' first dialogue with their children concerning sex is often sparked by the discovery of hidden contraceptives in the "children's" room.

♡ ♡ ♡

I wish my mom and dad would have been more open in this area. I feel if my parents were honest in telling me about sex, I would not have many fears and wrong information which I did as I was growing up hearing friends' experiences and very wrong morals.

♡ ♡ ♡

I had been told all my life that sex before marriage was wrong, but no one ever told me why. I had feelings of guilt, bitterness, hatred, jealousy, loneliness, frustration and filth. Due to those feelings, I would say to him, "We need to stop having sex or at least slow down." Well, we tried to slow down, but that did not work. Instead of getting closer, we grew farther apart.

After two years of dating I broke up with him, or should I say he broke up with me. I finally said, "No more sex," and he said, "Good-bye." Since then whenever I dated any one person for a length of time, sex became a part of the relationship. Tears always came because I knew that I had blown it again; and worse still, I didn't know why except for the fact that I was told so.

♡ ♡ ♡

I think that for you to develop convictions about sex, someone needs to teach you and train you about proper standards. Just saying "This is right and that is wrong" is not enough. You have to be trained and taught to be accountable for your actions.

And this is one area where practice hurts instead of helping. If you have to test your convictions by going against them, you've already blown it.

♡ ♡ ♡

I find that even now I'm so grateful for the things my parents told me not to do, because heaven only knows where I would be. Even though we make fun of them, we still heard it and we still remember it.

♡ ♡ ♡

My parents didn't realize when to start teaching me. They didn't realize I knew all about everything in the third grade. They figured they could wait until junior high — and then I explained it to them.

♡ ♡ ♡

I think it would help if parents could just take the time to understand how much of a good impact they could have by just stopping and showing the child in a caring and gentle way that premarital sex is a very serious thing and show how it could affect him, or just sit down and talk to him. I know it sure would be easier knowing that there was someone who could hold you accountable, who you knew really cared for you.

♡ ♡ ♡

Parents might be surprised how easy it is to talk to their children about it once they get started. You'll find they share some of the same values and ideas as you, but are just unsure of themselves.

♡ ♡ ♡

One reason for premarital sex was explained by one person, a young girl. This was, "My parents were always so hush-hush about it and made it seem so awful, I just had to see for myself. I wish that they would have told me that it was important to involve true love with it." She learned the hard way, but she promises to explain sex to her kids the right way before they end up hurt like she did.

———————————— ♥ ————————————

The following observation shows tremendous wisdom and perception about the need for the church to face the sex issue head-on in a positive, biblical way.

I think that the church as a whole has perverted the whole beautiful experience that sex is. Growing up in the church, you are conditioned to believe that sex is bad, wrong, and you do not talk about it openly. It is considered "taboo" to talk about sex outside the home, and even there it is not talked about that much. Sex is learned; and if it is not dealt with by parents, teachers, etc., then it will still be learned, but by events that you cannot control. The church puts a dark cloud over sex — they almost go to the extreme of presenting it as an unnatural act. This view comes from a virgin who is going to church and does not hate the church but sees a need for some basic change.

♡ ♡ ♡

19

Limits and Rules

*"Give me firm but reasonable limits and rules.
I may not admit it (or even realize it),
but I need boundaries to guide me."*

♥

Family psychologist Dick Day points out that within the family there needs to be a well-thought-through balance between love and limits or rules. When we encourage a child without accepting him, we put him on a performance basis. If we hold our children accountable without the relationship, then the old saying "rules without relationships lead to rebellion" becomes a reality. There needs to be: "I accept you; I love you; I encourage you"; but there also needs to be accountability. Then there is structural authority.

Most young people see the need for limits or boundaries to live within. This is balanced by their tremendous desire for an acceptance based on a love relationship with parents.

In the home, the authority that once existed seems to be vanishing at a rapid rate. Many parents, from what I have discovered from my peers, have not the slightest knowledge as to where their children spend their time or what they do with it. In the locker room it is not uncommon to hear someone say in laughter, "I'm going to John's to spend the night, but I told Mom I was staying with Jackie!" I feel most of these teens wish their parents loved them enough to say no more often. The freedom given readily by parents to children who wish to "think and decide for themselves what is best" allows the scene to be open wide for involvement with sex.

♡ ♡ ♡

I think one of the important reasons people become sexually active before marriage may be as simple as the word "parent." Too many parents let their children rule the house. They do not give teenagers the guidance and discipline that they ask for. I think of the many times my parents said no to me. I think it is one of the best things they have ever done for me. I wish the world was filled with parents like mine!

♡ ♡ ♡

Parents generally say you're not supposed to go all the way, but even if you accept that, you can get into a situation where you have gone so far that you may as well keep going. And parents don't address the in-between areas. So it's up to you to determine your own limits, but like I said, you might still wind up having sex if you do that. Parents need to be giving us specific guidelines, some real limits.

♡ ♡ ♡

I think my parents had a pretty good handle on the pressures I would be facing and helped keep me from them by not letting me do certain things (dances, parties with alcohol, socials, drive-in movies, etc.). At the time I felt it was terribly unfair and mean of them, but now looking back, I have not faced "pressure to have sex" from those types of situations.

♡ ♡ ♡

My parents taught me well. They were strict but it did teach me that my body was sacred to both God and the one man I would someday choose. Thanks, Mom and Dad!

───────────────── ♥ ─────────────────

"But don't lock me in a cage!"

The following comments show the other side of the coin of the preceding observations.

When from the eyes of the child there seems to be over-protection, then the parent needs to evaluate the situation. What the parent does may be seen from a different perspective by the child. Negative feelings need to be dealt with or they can compound with time. At this point the parent needs to take a good long realistic look at his relationship with the child, and if he has been overbearing, it might be good to back off the rules and work on the relationship. "Love" needs to be the foundation for "rules."

I wish my parents knew that I hate the over-protection they give me. I wish they wouldn't be so strict. I wish they would give me a little more freedom and responsibility — I haven't done anything to make them distrust me.

♡ ♡ ♡

Recently I heard about the strictness of a teenager's parents. They decided who she was to date, where she was to go, and who not to talk to when she got there. That, my friend, is provoking premarital sex.

♡ ♡ ♡

My dad and me are always at each other's throats because he won't let me grow up and he still kind of wants me as his little girl. It's hard. He really doesn't want me to go out with my friends; he still wants me to stay home and cook him dinner and all that stuff. It's hard to let him know that I can't always be there. I've got to grow up and do things on my own.

♡ ♡ ♡

Our parents went through different situations while they were growing up, and sometimes we have to go through the same things in order to grow up. They should let us get out and experience a few things instead of just saying "No, you can't go" because they think we'll do something wrong.

♡ ♡ ♡

I think our parents should give us more freedom. I have a friend who can't be out later than 10 P.M. so she just sneaks out and sneaks back in, because her parents don't let her do anything.

♡ ♡ ♡

20
Christian Teenagers

*"Don't think I can handle everything
just because I'm a Christian."*

♥

As parents we need to be careful that we don't take our kids' spirituality for granted. When an adolescent becomes a Christian, it not only adds a spiritual dimension to his life but also an intense moral conflict. A Christian teenager faces harder questions about sex than most non-Christians. They so need our love, prayer, support and encouragement for spiritual growth.

I was raised in a Christian home, but I felt like I got away with a lot and wish I was disciplined more.

♡ ♡ ♡

I'm not putting down my parents, but they think they've done too good a job. And I do know the Lord and have that and it does make a difference, but they don't think I'm tempted that much. Just because of the armor of the Lord, and the building blocks they've given me, they think I'm not tempted. They don't think I could ever be drunk either.

♡ ♡ ♡

I personally have often wondered what it would be like and sometimes that desire to go looking for a way to find out is hard to resist. And in our society I wouldn't have to look very far. One of the things that has helped me resist is that I've waited this long and it will still be around when I get married. But I still wonder sometimes if it would be worth it to go against God's will and try it now and ask for forgiveness later.

♡ ♡ ♡

Several years after becoming a Christian I began having sex with my boyfriend. It caused much guilt and eventually separated us, but before that I wound up pregnant and had to give my baby boy up for adoption.

♡ ♡ ♡

I had sexual intercourse with a man I did not know well and did not love. It was not lust or desire that sent me into this temptation and sin. I had felt unwanted and unloved and was spiritually lost. I had known the love of Jesus Christ, but it was not enough for me at the time.

♡ ♡ ♡

Although I am not proud of this fact, I had a very active sex life before becoming a Christian. It was an enjoyable part of my life, and although it was emotionally very ungratifying, it was hard to give up the physical gratification when I did become a

Christian. I've been a Christian for about 4 months now, and since that time I've fallen twice.

♡ ♡ ♡

When I became a Christian, I had a fear of saying no, because I wanted to be loving toward the guy. And as he pushed those things on me, I didn't want to say no. I didn't know how to deal with that situation, 'cause nobody ever told me.

♡ ♡ ♡

Christians have a lot of the same peer pressure on them in some ways, but they always have Christ to turn to when they really feel it. Sometimes guys pressure you more because they know you have convictions and they want to see you "loosen up," and other times they'll just leave you alone because they know you're a Christian.

But Christians always know that if they do something with a girl and word gets around, their witness is shot. That's an extra pressure.

♡ ♡ ♡

"I will stay a virgin till I'm married," is the famous phrase of many teens, Christian and non-Christian alike, as they embark on the wonderful journey of finding out who they really are and what they really stand for in an unfair world full of broken promises and seasonal satisfaction. As a teenager raised in a Christian home, by spirit-filled parents who love Jesus, I had the same desire as so many others to save myself for the husband God had waiting for me. Yet even with this conviction I, like so many others, fell victim to the lies, the false freedom, and momentary feelings premarital sex offered.

♡ ♡ ♡

It is hard even for a Christian guy to relate to a girl without thinking of her in sexual terms. Often the sexual obsession is an attempt to make up for intimacy you miss when you badly want a good relationship with your parents. Usually a guy will make love with a girl to have sex, and the girl will have sex to make love. It's a trap that is very hard to get out of. I face this experience daily.

♡ ♡ ♡

I look back on that past relationship and I could kick myself. I wish it had never happened. I do not understand how I could give myself to someone who did not have my values. I know today that I am a special person and that God made me in His image and likeness. I cannot give that gift to just anyone.

♡ ♡ ♡

If my parents understood the conflict I feel about sexuality and its pressures, they could help me to resist temptation and obey the Word of God and His message against premarital sex. We as youth could learn to trust, to believe and to love people the way God intends us to. In 1 Corinthians 6:18 it states: "Flee fornication. Every sin that a man doeth is without the body; but he that committeth fornication sinneth against his own body" (KJV). I want to do what's right and so do most teenagers. The problem is we don't always know how. Help us!

♡ ♡ ♡

21

"God Bless You Both"

*"I don't say it enough, but I love you
more than anything in the world."*

---♥---

The teens' comments throughout the essays highlighted the need and desire for family life. Research shows that one of the greatest desires of a teenager today is for a happy home life. So much in a teen's world centers around, is conditioned by, or stems from, the family in both a positive and a negative sense.

Dr. Billy Graham captures this vital link between a child and his or her family. He writes in the Foreword to the priceless parent resource book, *Parents and Teenagers:*

> Young people have always had growing pains, but today the problems are often deeper, more intense, and more complex. Suddenly teenagers — and their parents — find themselves facing a host of problems that were seldom encountered a generation or so ago. Teenagers are searching for identity, meaning in life, purpose, direction. Buffeted by a host of pressures from their peers and their society, they're rewriting the scripts of their lives, headed in a multitude of directions — and often running into serious trouble in the process.

Why is this so? I am convinced the basic answer lies in the rapid and severe erosion of family life today. The family is one of the most fundamental means God uses to communicate with us and shape us. In this modern information age, we know that when communication lines are broken, confusion results. Likewise, when the family breaks down, confusion and chaos are inevitable. God's pattern for the family becomes twisted and distorted.[1]

Many parents, though, have understood this problem and have been able to come to grips with it. And their young people are well aware of the positive influences their parents have had. Here are some letters from some grateful teenagers. Consider especially the first one — words from a young man who in a few sentences has summed up the feelings of thousands of these teenagers:

You might think you know me inside and out, but you really don't. Just as you matured into an independent person through your experiences and lessons, so I am maturing through a different set of experiences and lessons.

Please understand that I'm not your little child anymore, but then again I'm not totally independent either. I'm becoming a separate person, so I don't need you to hold my hand anymore.

I need you to light the way through your love and example. I need your prayers through this time called puberty, as I'm beginning to discover the beauty of the opposite sex, not only physically, but also the beauty of the inside — that's what counts.

And please, Mom, don't be jealous when I fall in love. No one can take your place. The woman who will eventually become my bride will be someone to enhance my life and make it richer, not someone to lessen my love for you. No one sent from God could diminish my love for another person, especially you.

Mom and Dad, God bless you both.

♡ ♡ ♡

I believe I will always be able to keep problems in perspective because my parents have taught me how to communicate and deal with problems. I would like to thank them for being godly parents and for supporting me in all I have done.

♡ ♡ ♡

I was very lucky growing up with two wonderful parents. They made every effort they could to make me understand and have a good attitude about sexuality. Often, their main topic of jokes and laughter were things to do with sex. They were very conservative and believed (and still do) that sex must only occur in marriage.

When I was 14, my 19-year-old sister became pregnant. My parents hit the ceiling. It was about two months before they realized it was going to happen, she would have a baby. After the reality hit, they became very loving and understanding. That showed me a lot about who they were. They never once said they thought it was right, yet they loved her just as much, and the child the same.

♡ ♡ ♡

My parents' marriage is such an example of how I want my marriage to be one day. My parents have always been there when I needed them. They have always given each other and me a lot of love. My parents are my best friends and I love them.

♡ ♡ ♡

I love both of my parents very much. I've always felt lucky to have parents who will stop whatever they're doing to listen to or be with *me*. I am the oldest of four kids and I know I am loved very, very much. Some of my friends' parents don't pay much attention to their kids so my friends always feel kind of alone. I am very understanding with others and I don't criticize them or put them down. I am just *so* glad I am loved!

♡ ♡ ♡

I want to thank my parents for helping me through relationships with friends. If it wasn't for my parents, I would probably have killed myself two years ago when I had a very bad self-image and was hanging out with the wrong crowd. But my parents stayed with me through it all and helped me back to Christ. Thanks, Mom and Dad!

♡ ♡ ♡

Thank you for being examples of godly parents and keeping communication within the family so open that I can share *everything* with you.

♡ ♡ ♡

Mom and Dad — I don't say it enough, but I love you more than anything in the world. You care for me and try to point me in the right direction. When I end up in big trouble you still care about me and have never given up on me.

♡ ♡ ♡

I want to tell you how thankful I am that you have been such great Christian examples for me. You have always been so unselfish and put my wants and needs before your own. I am very proud to say you are my parents because you have integrity and real Christian love. Thank you for teaching me the true principles of life and for the way you raised me.

♡ ♡ ♡

Thanks for all the support you've given me in my endeavors. Thanks, Dad, for being a good provider. Thanks, Mom, for watching me and being by my side.

♡ ♡ ♡

I wish you knew how much I love you, especially for loving me even when I caused you so much pain. I've always loved you deeply, but there was a time when my desire for self-gratification over-shadowed my love for you. Now I can see how hard it must have been to love me through those times and that your love never diminished despite every-thing. You will probably never know how much I love you for holding on to me even then. Thank you and thank God for such loving parents.

♡ ♡ ♡

Regardless of whether sexual expression is permit-ted me at some future date, I will always be grateful for friends and family alike who have contributed to my realization of the one part of my being that adds up to a total life experience. Just the chance to say, "I love you," and to touch someone in a tender way will be worth all the wait even if it were to take ten thousand years!!!!

♥

I couldn't have said it better myself!

22

Communicating
With Teenagers

*"Honey, you need to spend
a little more time listening. . ."*

♥

"Do you know what I am?" a teenager once asked.
"I'm a comma."

"What do you mean?" the listener replied.

He said, "Whenever I talk to my dad, he stops
talking and makes a comma. Then when I stop talking,
he starts right up again as if I didn't say anything. I'm
just a comma in the middle of his speeches."

Many of our young people are crying out for a
real conversation with a parent. One that involves not
only the exchange of thoughts, but also feelings. A
conversation that involves both a listener and a talker.

The same principles that apply to adult communication apply to adult-teen conversations. However, the
difficulty arises out of fear of rejection or ridicule. A
child often will be hesitant to share his real feelings
or opinions. Who wants to feel ridiculed or rejected?
Who has a chance to win an argument with an adult?

A priority principle in communicating with your
child is that rules without relationships lead to rebellion.

I've seen it happen over and over again. A child does something morally wrong, and the parents say, "How could this happen? We've clearly taught her what the Bible teaches about that kind of behavior." You can have all the rules you want in a family, but if you don't have relationships with your children, you are going to have rebellion instead of response.

Good relationships are built on mutual respect. If you respect your children's rights, they will respect yours. Respect begins with listening. If you feel that someone is listening to you, you feel respected. Shakespeare said in *Hamlet,* "Give every man your ear but seal your tongue." James said in the New Testament, "Be quick to listen, slow to speak" (1:19, NIV). An Irish proverb says, "God gave us two ears and one mouth, so we ought to listen twice as much as we speak."

We parents tend to treat our children's problems too lightly. "Oh, you'll get over it," we'll say. I've found that children take their problems just as seriously as you or I take ours. Their problems may not go as deep as ours, but they don't have as much experience as we do either. So that means that emotionally, we're at the same place when we face problems.

We need to be careful that we in no way make light of our children's problems. When they are facing difficulties, we have a unique opportunity to influence them. We can hug them, encourage them, share from our own experience, or walk through the problem with them. Often we don't need to say anything at all. It is tempting to step in and start giving sermonettes, but listening is usually more important. The children often just want a sympathetic ear, a sounding board.

An important part of communicating is to hear the children out. This is where I fall short. I always want to interrupt, not to wait for the whole story. But kids want to give you the whole situation, and if they feel you are not going to hear them out, they will clam up. You might get a few facts, but you won't get their feelings.

We parents seem to feel we need to give advice, to quote the Bible to our children, when often we just need to listen. A teenager said to me recently, "You know, I try to share something with my parents and as soon as I open my mouth, they start quoting the Bible. I don't want the Bible quoted; I just want them to listen to me."

Concentration on what our children are saying can be difficult. For every 100 words spoken, we can hear and understand 500, so it's easy for the mind to wander. I keep saying to myself, "Can you repeat back to your child what he or she is saying?" If I keep that thought running through my mind, it helps me concentrate. Part of good communication is listening with the eyes as well as with the ears. Look for physical and non-verbal communication — the way your children use their eyes, the gestures they make. If you don't watch for nonverbal cues, you're missing part of their communication.

Some parents are quite ready to listen, but their teenage children won't talk. How can they encourage the kids to open up?

First, parents need to enter the children's world enough so that they are speaking the same language. They need to get their children's perspective. I'm forty-four years old, and it's hard for me to get back to junior high and know exactly what I was going through. Still, I'm constantly trying to see my children's viewpoints. I want to know their world, and I must know it if I am going to communicate with them. I need to listen to their music, read what they read, know their friends, understand their frustrations, laugh at their jokes. I also need to consider how what I say will affect them. They may not take things the same way an adult would, so I need to look at my statements to them from their perspective. Communication takes a lot of work!

Communicating with my children is easier if we are involved together in something they enjoy — surfing, soccer, basketball, jogging, cooking. We had two acres of ground that we weren't using, so we built a soccer field on it. I set up and poured a basketball court behind the garage. I have a friend who took a class with three of his kids every Thursday night for a term. It became the central topic of household discussion. They did their homework together, and Thursday mornings they would go out to breakfast together to discuss what they studied. I thought that was fantastic.

It is imperative to take the time to listen. Dr. Norman Wright, founder and director of Family Counseling and Enrichment, and Christian Marriage Enrichment, both in Santa Ana, California, writes about finding time to listen:

> "This is not a good time," we may tell our kids when they want to talk. "I'm fixing dinner. I'm tired. Come back another time."
>
> But maybe we adults have more control over our time than our teens have over theirs. With school, extracurricular activities, part-time jobs, and dating, our kids may not have much time left. Maybe we parents need to break out of our time structures and be available when our teens are.
>
> That's not easy. We get so tied up in our frustrations that we may think, "Nobody listens to *me* around here. I'm not going to listen to *them.*" But for parents who realize the importance of listening, the question becomes, "What am I doing with my time, and why am I doing it? Is it really more important than having time with my son or daughter?"[1]

Then, parents who want to encourage their teens to talk must obey certain ground rules. With teenagers, especially, it's important to be able to keep secrets. If I go out and tell others a secret my teens have shared with me, I'm going to destroy their confidence in me.

It's also important to be open about one's faults. My children may not remember all the times I've been kind to people, but they will remember the times I lost my temper. If I try to cover up my failures, I won't fool my children. I'll just teach them to keep their tracks covered too. Instead of hiding my faults, I should confess them and use them as lessons for both myself and my children.

When things are going right with my children, I sometimes share negative things out of my childhood, like frustrations I had with my father and how we worked them through. God's Holy Spirit plants those things in their minds, and then when they go through similar frustrations, they remember them without feeling like I'm preaching to them.

Kids really respond to praise and encouragement. I try to praise my kids at least twenty-five times a day. I'm constantly going out of my way looking for ways to praise my children. I tell them what a good job they did, or how nice they look. If I use criticism and sarcasm, I get a reaction, but if I give praise and encouragement, I get a response. Touching and hugging is another key to reaching children, even after they become teenagers. Hug them when they hurt, hug them when joyful, hug them for the fun of it.

With teenagers, as with anyone else, one way to get communication going is to ask questions. If I don't plan ahead and ask questions, I usually talk only about things that interest me. But if I ask specific questions, the children end up talking about their own concerns. When they come home from school, I ask, "Did you do anything special? What didn't you like today?" I try to bring out feelings as well as facts. "How did you feel when your friend told you he'd cheated?"

Something that has really helped me communicate with my kids is to ask their opinions. Not only do I get a lot of good information that way, but I also communicate to them that they are important to me and that what they have to say is important. Several years ago when I was preparing some talks on forgiveness, I got my children and a friend's children together at breakfast and asked their help. The children made a list of reasons that some people are unwilling to confess their sins to God and receive forgiveness. They gave me good ideas, and they also became a part of my ministry. They still talk about that experience today.

My wife, an exceptional woman with tremendous ability to listen and communicate, is a barometer for me. She'll say, "Honey, you need to spend a little more time with Sean, listening to him." Or, "You know, Kelly wanted to say something to you this afternoon, and you didn't really listen to her. I think maybe you need to go into her room." If I don't know quite how to respond to one of the children, sometimes I'll say, "Let's ask Mother to come in here. Let's see what she has to say." My wife plays a major role in maintaining good communication in our family. Much of what I've learned, I've learned from her.

Fathers as well as mothers need to take communication with their children seriously. I once did a week-long conference at a large evangelical church. Apart from my speaking, I had forty-two personal appointments with junior high and high school students who wanted counseling. I asked each one of these kids, "Can you talk with your father?" Only one said yes. The number one question I kept getting from these students was this: "Josh, what can I do about my dad?

He never talks to me; he never takes me anywhere; he never does anything with me."

If we parents make talking with our children a number one priority, it will rub off on them and they will make a priority of talking with us. I've found that I need to plan ahead if I'm going to have a good discussion with my family. My wife and I sometimes plan discussion topics for the dinner table. Other good times for communication include riding to school — an excellent time to discuss their likes and dislikes, their feelings, what they are going to be doing that day — and riding to church.

I like to take a child with me when I make a trip into town. Recently I had to drive to Ramona, a little over twenty miles from our home, so I took my three-and-a-half-year-old daughter along for the ride. Ahead of time, I thought through five or six questions to discuss with her. If I hadn't planned, we wouldn't have had that discussion. The time would have just slipped by.

Some of the most intimate times between parents and children can take place in their rooms or in the master bedroom. There is a different feeling if you are in their territory or they are in yours. And bedtime, of course, is an excellent time to communicate. But once again, I find that if I don't think ahead about what I'm going to say, I don't say anything.

It's easy to let the day's pressures crowd out precious time for communicating with our children. One day I was under tremendous pressure to finish a book that I'd promised the publisher. I had stayed up all night working on it. Then my son came in and wanted to talk. I knew he had been upset by a visit to the doctor, who had commented about his small stature, but I would not have chosen that moment to discuss it.

"Josh," I said to myself, "you're going to have pressure deadlines the rest of your life. You're always going to have work to do, but you're not always going to have a hurting child to talk to. Take advantage of the opportunity." So I just pushed my stuff aside and spent the next half hour talking with him about his shortness, the fact that he's unique and that God made him that way, and the advantages and disadvantages of being short.

Sometimes, of course, I just can't talk to the child when he wants my attention. Too often I used to say, "Honey, I can't talk right now," and then when I was free it was too late to help. I've found that it's best to say, "You know, Son, I want to discuss this with you, but I can't right now. If you will come back at such and such a time, then I'll be free and I'll give you my full attention." I've found that my children have a whole different attitude when I do that. They don't feel that they are being shoved aside, that I'm not interested in them.

If we parents show an interest in our children when they're young, they will show an interest in us later. Good communication with teenagers requires a lot of time and thought, but it is the foundation of a lifelong family relationship.

For further reading on how to keep the communication lines clear and to be a better communicator, see the Resources section at the end of the book, and see especially chapters 4 and 5 of *The Secret of Loving*.[2]

SECTION III
Sex: To Have Or Not To Have

23

51 Reasons for Sex

♥

This list of reasons teens get involved in sex was gleaned from thousands of their startlingly honest responses.

1. A sign of maturity (shows passage from childhood to adulthood).

Many young people, even though they are still in school, view themselves as fully mature. Because of this feeling, they want to engage in so-called adult activities such as smoking, drinking and having sex. It would be tough to explain to them why they shouldn't involve themselves in sex if they see themselves as adults and then look around them and see what other adults are doing. Another group may want to have sex to become mature. They think if they have sex, they will somehow magically become adults.

2. "It is cool."

Things began to snowball and we were all beginning to indulge in drugs, alcohol, and premarital sex. One of our nights out would be to go over to someone's house, drink, smoke some pot, and then go to our own separate rooms. It was almost a ritual, a habit. When it came right down to it, I didn't really enjoy it. It was gross to think that my friends were in the next room or sometimes in the same room having sex. There were no feelings at all, not for each other and not for ourselves. We were basically doing it because it was cool. . .

3. "It feels good."

Where I live, many of my girl friends and guy friends are involved in sex because they just want to do it. I asked them, "Why?" Most said it makes them feel good. . .

4. Modeled by environment and society.

"Sinfully Sexy — Fourteen Red-Hot Men"; "The Intelligent Woman's Guide to Sex"; "Orgasms — Real or Fake?" These are just a few of the article titles in some of today's most popular magazines. The sexuality of today's society affects today's unmarried people like no other time in history. Our society has become obsessed with the topic of sexuality, which has become central to almost everything we, as Americans, do with our spare time.

5. Confusion and disillusionment.

The average teenager today is confused and disillusioned. Virtually every relationship has stabbed him in the back. He wonders, *Who can I trust?* The big difference between this generation and the rebellious generations before is that the rebellion before was for a cause. This generation has no cause. They have given up. They have no vision.

6. Broken homes.

Some 67 percent of today's teens come from broken homes. Teenagers' attitudes were developed mostly when they were children. Sometimes, unfortunately, children grow up to be like their parents. Broken homes cause instability and the inability to make wise decisions.

7. Lack of guidelines and restrictions.

A majority of teens desperately want guidelines and restrictions. Ask a teenager if he wants rules, and he will probably laugh at you. However, deep inside, he wants someone in authority to say "no further." Yet no one does. Consequently, he is his own god.

8. Search for reality.

They are searching for reality. A real person is one who lives the truth as well as speaks it. Many teens believe parents are hypocrites, ministers are hypocrites, and friends are hypocrites. Every voice they hear lies to them, so whom do they trust?

9. Search for identity, security and acceptance

For instance, a girl's family is really having problems and she needs someone to listen to her, care about her, and most of all love her. In her eyes, she needs someone who will just make her forget about all of her problems, someone she can hold on to for

Vicious circle of premarital sex

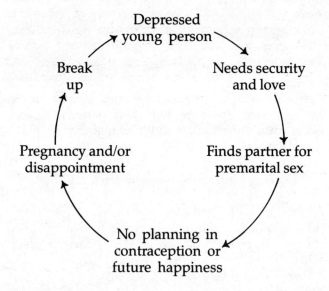

security. She meets the "perfect guy" to her, but really this guy is having basically the same problems and is looking for security as well. Neither one of them knowing what real love is, they may mistake it for sex. This is where a lot of people my age get into trouble.

10. Peer pressure.

Friends tease and pressure to the point of humiliating the virgin girl for not having sex. Peers call them prudes or nerds or even go so far as to call them homosexuals because of their refusal to have premarital sex. Some will give in just to prove that they are as normal as the next person.

11. Lack of understanding of what real love is.

Teens misunderstand what real love is. Today's teenagers think love is an act instead of a commitment. Ninety percent of all guys and eighty percent of all girls will lose their virginity by age twenty. They have no example before them of real love and many have been taught sex education without morals from grade school up.

12. Easy access to birth control devices.

The most common reason for saying no to premarital sex was the risk of the female involved getting pregnant. The risk was simply too high, and the chances for an unwanted pregnancy stopped most from having sex before marriage. However, we now live in the eighties. Medical science has more than effectively killed the risk of an unwanted baby. The male can use creams to render himself sterile for a short time period, and if the girl thinks ahead she can use birth control pills. Any pharmacy and most drug stores sell these and other less "sure" ways of preventing pregnancy. For the woman who was not smart enough to use preventative medicine there is now abortion as an option. Virtually all major cities in the United States have clinics where a woman or girl can receive an abortion to rid herself of an unwanted baby. If the woman did not prevent the pregnancy and is against abortion, she can give the child up for adoption.

13. Curiosity.

Although each individual feels his reason is different, there are three general ideas as to why people start and continue a sex life: curiosity, acceptance, and different morals. With all the movies, TV shows, books, and people portraying lifestyles caught up in sex and making the act of intercourse something unsurpassingly exhilarating, it is no wonder that anyone would be curious. "What does it feel like?" "Is it really as wonderful as they say?" "If it's not as wonderful, then not everyone would want to do it, right?" These are just some of the questions which crop up due to wonderment.

14. Sex education without standards.

Sex education is taught in detail without any standards. When the book says an orgasm feels great, it makes a person want to go and see how great it really feels. When you know a little you are confident, but you actually know enough to be dangerous. *Psychology Today* tells people that they could solve the pregnancy problem if they would teach more and at a younger age . . . brilliant!

15. A thrill.

Teenagers are bored. Technology has provided them with so much passive entertainment — television, video games, etc. — that the ordinary, God-given, wholesome things in life have no meaning. LIFE is boring! No thrills, no challenges . . . so . . . create your own thrills!

16. Pressure from boyfriend or girl friend.

This pressure is harder not to succumb to because we're dealing with someone we really care about. Teenagers feel they owe their partner some sort of allegiance, and feel obligated to have sex with them. They also feel that if their partner wants to have sex, and they object, their partner is going to break up with them or something.

17. Feel the need/desire to be loved.

In many cases there is only one parent, or if both parents are together, the relationship is not that great. Teenagers feel the need to be loved and cared for and a lot of them are not receiving the love and attention needed. They do not feel they fit in anywhere; they are looking for love in all the wrong places. They are trying to belong somewhere. Sadly enough they turn to sex thinking they are receiving love, but usually they end up adding to their hurt.

18. Lack of information.

Lack of accurate information about sex, although less of a problem than in our parents' adolescence, is still quite common, and young people often don't realize how far they are going. Before they know it, they have an unexpected pregnancy on their hands. It must be pointed out that some parents are to blame on the grounds that they have not informed their children on the topic of sex, either because they are embarrassed to discuss it or are too feckless to regard it as a parental responsibility.

19. Fear.

Some people become sexually active not out of need, but out of fear. What are the fears which may cause a person to lean toward a premature sexual relationship? There is the fear of physical deterioration and emotional abnormality. There is the fear that time is running out. Another fear may be that of losing a treasured relationship. And there is a common fear in our crowded world today and that is loneliness. Yes, there are a variety of reasons why people get sexually involved, but often the means does not bring the desired result.

20. An expression of love.

Infatuation is why I got sucked into premarital sex. My "first love" was two years older than I was and because we loved each other and were "going to be married someday," the whole idea of losing our virginity to one another seemed so romantic and so right at the time.

21. The result of a mind being filled with impure thoughts.

I do not believe that most Christians make a single, willful decision to commit fornication. Rather, it is a series of smaller decisions which allow for improper thinking to enter in. Once the mind has been contaminated with impure thoughts and desires, it becomes much easier for us to make wrong decisions. The solution is to make preliminary decisions concerning sexual activities that preclude ever arriving at a place where questions of a more serious nature can be asked. That is to say that if I make a commitment to never allow myself to be in a dark room with a soft couch with a beautiful girl alone, I will never have to contend with the question of whether it is OK for us to have sex.

22. Drinking or drugs causing one to let his or her guard down.

Another factor which contributes to promiscuous behavior is drug and alcohol abuse. Drugs and alcohol cloud judgment and distort the emotions. Both of these substances are rampant in adolescent society today. In my peer group sex often does not occur without one or the other.

23. To prepare for sexual compatibility in marriage.

Some reasons people engage in premarital sex are that they believe courtship quarreling comes from a couple not having sex and that many brides who enter marriage as virgins are afraid of sex. Both of these reasons are illogical. Most quarrels are a result of insecurity, selfishness and jealousy. Also most girls are not afraid of sex but of premarital pregnancy, immorality and an unsuccessful marriage.

24. To prove love.

People also worry about offending their girl friend or boyfriend. For example, the boy may believe that having sex is the only way for the girl to prove her love. If the girl doesn't have sex with him, it would be the same as saying that she doesn't love him. Even though to her this isn't true, her boyfriend may believe this. When this situation arises, the girl has to decide who is more important to her, God or her boyfriend. The other solution would be for her boyfriend to change and realize that a good relationship is more important than having sex.

25. The feeling that no one will be hurt, so why not?

Although the promiscuous lifestyle of the '60s is no longer in vogue, the popularity of sex before marriage is still on the rise. And why should we be surprised? Not only is sex a pleasurable experience, but with the proper care, two can be reasonably sure children will not result and disease will be avoided. So, if nobody is hurt, why wait till marriage?

26. Economic pressures.

In our culture, it is not uncommon for a person to be in his middle-to-late twenties before marriage can be afforded. How can we argue against premarital sex when the number of years between physical sexual development and potential marriage is so great?

27. Negative perception of what God wants for us.

The third obstacle to the discussion of Christian arguments against premarital sex is theological, and has to do with our negative perception of what God wants for us. Many Christians don't believe that God wants good things for them. At some level, people often feel that His commands are there to deprive them or hold them down. We need to hear Christ's answer to His own rhetorical questions in the Sermon on the Mount:

> Which of you, if his son asks for bread, will give him a stone? Or if he asks for a fish, will give him a snake? If you, then, though you are evil, know how to give good gifts to your children, how much more will your Father in heaven give good gifts to those who ask him! (Matthew 7:9-11, NIV).

28. Fear of rejection or of getting hurt.

Today's teens are faced with a decision that will affect them the rest of their lives. If they choose to give in, the outcome may destroy them. If they choose to stand steadfast and not give in, they may still feel temporary effects of rejection or loss of self-esteem.

29. "Everyone else is doing it."

Why wait? I have asked myself that question many times during my first 23 years. Why must everyone else have all the fun, and me, yes me, I had to be the odd ball . . . the one who wouldn't do this, couldn't do that . . . after all, where was all this purity getting me? Why couldn't I give of myself and my love freely?

30. Seems natural.

I feel that the main force driving people in my age group into having premarital sex is the view of society that sex is only natural. With this kind of atmosphere, people don't see the need to hold out until they are married.

31. "It's OK — we're engaged."

Many people feel if they are engaged, they can go ahead and have sex. They feel if they are going to be married, why not just have sex a little earlier?

32. In order not to lose boyfriend or girl friend.

A lot of my friends tell me about how their boy-friends want them to do sexually active things. When a girl's boyfriend asks her to do sexual things, she's afraid to say no. She thinks by saying no her boyfriend will not want to continue their relationship.

33. Boosts the ego.

The fact that he was older than me at this age played a big part too. I was so in awe that a 17-year-old could be attracted to a 15-year-old that it boosted my ego and I felt mature enough for sex.

34. Longing for spiritual oneness.

From a female point of view, I know that the spiritual oneness and not the physical oneness is the main reason girls today long for sexual union.

35. Loneliness.

What most people think is a desire for sex can be loneliness. Since many people think having sex brings an intimacy that can't be received from anything else, they feel this is the only way to escape their loneliness.

36. To escape problems or sense of failure.

One of the reasons that is overlooked the most is that of pressure. Not the pressure of friends, either. I'm talking about the pressure of having to get good grades, make a certain athletic team, go out with a certain girl, plan a post high school career. The list goes on and on. The problem is that some teens find themselves not performing up to everyone else's standards and this reflects on them and then they feel like they're not capable of doing a certain thing. As this vicious cycle progresses, the one thing a

teen can do is have sex, whether it be to release
tension or to give a sense of doing something right
or succeeding at something.

37. Search for intimacy.

Another reason he might rush into sex is that he
is anxious to push this relationship into maturity in
his search for intimacy. When they are making out
it gives him such a sense of security and he "knows"
that they really are starting to get close.

38. Tired of waiting.

Many people become sexually active because they
are tired of waiting on God to bring the right person
into their lives. Many people, therefore, feel cheated
by God in the area of sex. This is true for many
single Christians who are striving to honor God in
the area of sexual purity.

39. Fear of never getting married.

They may lose hope in the future possibility of
ever finding a compatible mate. These thoughts can
be reinforced especially in a person who never dated
much or conversely by the person who dated often
and never seemed to find the right person.

Another reason for premarital sex would be a loss
of hope in finding a permanent partner in a world
where people and things are always changing. This
can lead to a "live for now" or "get it while I can"
mentality.

40. Music.

Lyrics in contemporary rock and even country music are a bit too suggestive and talk a little too freely on the topic of sex. Some songs have lyrics that talk about such things as one-night love affairs, part-time lovers, this night will be a night of magic, and the list goes on. Some teenagers may think nothing of it and say, "Oh, I don't listen to the words, I just like the rhythm and the tune." Subconsciously, they may take in some of those suggestive lyrics. From this, they may think that sex is all right, which is not good.

41. Frustration of waiting.

I recall many of my Christian friends envying non-Christians who would pick up the best-looking cheerleader or the beautiful model and engage in heavy sex. Proverbs 23:17 says: "Do not let your heart envy sinners, but live in the fear of the LORD always" (NASB). The frustration of "Why do I have to wait, Lord? I want the experience of sex now!" is found in a lot of single men and women in the 20- to 30-year age category.

I find people, therefore, continually being frustrated in the waiting process for God to bring Mr. or Mrs. Right into the picture. People are simply burned out on waiting. This is why trying to find a virgin in my age category is sometimes like trying to find a needle in a haystack.

42. Skepticism about commitment.

Another reason for sex before marriage would be a personal choice not to be married due to a distrust of marriage, lack of commitment, or being the child of a divorce. This person might choose to become involved in short-term relationships, or in a long-term relationship which does not include marriage but does include sex. Another reason would be the lack of the ability to make an emotional commitment to another person, and using sex for personal gratification.

43. "I've done it once; why not do it again?"

Adolescents sometimes believe that once they've participated in sexual activity, there's no use in stopping because you've already messed up and there's no way you can change that. This is a common feeling.

44. Rebellion.

The problem today is that teenagers are being given information earlier, and accompanying it is this message from the world: "If it feels good, do it." At the same time they are receiving God's message from parents, church or others: "Do not show or express these feelings and emotions yet." This type of thing tears the mind apart as they try to decide what to do and who they should really listen to. Many teenagers will react to what God wants them to do just as Eve did in the Garden of Eden by saying, "I don't care what God wants me to do; I know better!"

45. Feeling that it's owed to the other person.

Another reason could be that you feel like you owe it to your boyfriend or girl friend. Perhaps they have been really nice to you, and you think sex could repay them. First, your date or steady is probably nice to you because they want to be. Second, you don't owe them anything. If they try to say you do, that's probably the only reason they were being nice to you in the first place. You have to stick to your own personal morals; you don't owe sex to anyone.

46. No self-control.

Some people have sex because they have a weak body and mind. They don't have the will power to say no. Once they are kissing and petting, they can't stop themselves.

47. Television.

Many teenage girls and even a few boys are hooked on "soap operas." In most soap operas almost every person in the cast is involved with sex before they are married. Teenagers watch this and they are told through these programs that premarital sex will cause you to be content and happy.

48. Law of diminishing returns.

Basically, the physical aspect of any relationship should be paced, i.e., "the ladder of affection." It innocently starts with a look, then touch, holding hands, kiss, then after quite some time (engagement believed by some), the French kiss, and then the progression into intercourse.

49. Boredom.

Boredom is another possible reason which explains a teen's need to engage in sex. Teenagers all around the globe complain that they have nothing to do. So instead of finding something to do, they find boyfriends and girl friends to occupy their time. They don't seem to understand that time could be better spent, possibly helping others instead of hindering their own lives. Boredom, although it can be claimed as a reason, is no excuse for doing something morally wrong.

50. They can't say no.

"NO!" Why is this word, one of the smallest and easiest to say in our English language, so hard to say when it comes to premarital sex among teenagers? I feel that so many teens who pass me in the halls at school engage in premarital sex because they won't say NO!

51. Absence of a sense of morality and obedience.

I was watching "Family Ties" one morning, and the issue of the episode was whether the sixteen-year-old daughter should sleep with her eighteen-year-old boyfriend. She asked her friends for advice, and one warned her that if she didn't sleep with him, she would lose him. Another friend advised that if she decided to go through with it, she'd better be sure to get birth control pills and that it wouldn't be very romantic for a sixteen-year-old to be pregnant. The third friend advised her not to go through with it at all. When she asked her brother for advice, he tried to convince her not to because she was too young. He believed in the double standard, that when a guy loses his virginity, he is a "winner," but if a girl loses hers, she should be ashamed. Her mother told her that it was a matter of whether she was ready for it.

The daughter decided she wasn't ready and didn't go through with it. She made the right decision by choosing not to engage in premarital sex, but her ever-so-complicated decision wasn't based on anything solid. She looked to the world for advice and gave no account to morals found in the Bible.

24

47 Reasons to Wait

♥

These reasons to wait for sex until marriage were taken directly from the responses submitted to the "Write Your Heart Out" essay contest.

1. God commands us to be pure.

The first reason we should wait is that God commands us to. As you know, when God sets rules or standards for us, He isn't trying to frustrate us. After all, He is the one who created us and He has *our* best interest in mind. With this in mind, let's look at what God's Word has to say concerning this matter. In 1 Thessalonians 4:3, Paul writes: "For this is the will of God, your sanctification; that is, that you abstain from sexual immorality" (NASB). And in 1 Corinthians 6:13 it says: "Yet the body is not for immorality, but for the Lord; and the Lord is for the body" (NASB). This says that the Lord is for us and sets down guidelines for us because He loves us. He knows that the only way for us to experience love and sex to the fullest is in a marriage relationship.

God commands us to wait because He has our best interest in mind.

2. Premarital sex can make future courtship much more difficult.

The Christian sees courtship as a critical period of time; the potential stakes involved are the many years of a presumably lifelong marriage. In view of the tremendous investment a lifelong relationship represents, many aspects of a relationship need to be worked out before a commitment is made.

3. Waiting allows freedom to develop strong friendships.

Some have chosen celibacy because of the health danger of indiscriminate sex in our society. But the majority seem to have chosen celibacy because after having become involved in sexual relationships, they found themselves empty and unable to respond emotionally any longer. Most of those interviewed said they got involved to meet emotional needs such as for closeness and self-worth, and needing to be involved with another human being. But the end result was to lose their ability to give emotionally or to even feel much at all. Men as well as women stated that the emotional toll was not worth the sex.

Most of those interviewed have turned instead to building strong friendships instead of love affairs. They found their needs for human interaction and involvement being met without using sex. They now find the freedom to become friends with the opposite sex instead of just sleeping with them. All in all, they feel much better about themselves and about being able to cope with life.

4. Premarital sex takes away the specialness of sex in marriage.

I never realized that I felt cheated until my wedding night when we got to our hotel room. As I was getting ready for the most romantic evening of my life, I looked in the mirror and realized I had already done this. What a letdown! What was there to be excited about? This was nothing new. I felt like all the life had been drained out of me. That was the final deadening of the poison in my heart!

As the months went on we got frustrated and uptight. Sex used to be so much fun before we got married. What happened?

Sex was just a game before and then when it should have been the ultimate expression of love between a husband and wife it had no meaning!

We struggled with it for almost a year. We had that ugly root of unforgiveness between us and the sin between us and the Lord. It was about to destroy us, so we went to some close friends and received counseling, prayer, and forgiveness from the Lord. Now things are as they should be.

5. God has set sex aside for the marriage relationship.

The first reason is to increase our joy in the marriage relationship. God wants two virgins, free from guilt or shame, to enter into marriage undefiled. God does not want people burdened down with emotional scars entering into marriage. God desires two people that are so committed to God's rules for marriage, that they will abstain from premarital sex, and enter into marriage with the certainty of each other's purity. That is definitely joy!

6. Sexually transmitted diseases are dangerous.

In discussing AIDS, an article written by Dr. Janice Hopkins Tanne in *Readers Digest* states, "The greatest risk for most men and women is sex. Even a discriminative person can't know a new partner's sexual history or whether the person has tried intravenous drugs."[1] In this same article Dr. George D. Lundbey, editor of the *Journal of the American Medical Association*, was quoted as saying, "People who do not wish to get AIDS must adjust their lifestyle so as to live defensively. This is a great time to practice sexual monogamy." In the book, *Questions Patients Most Often Ask Their Doctors*, Dr. Lester R. Hibbard, M.D., Professor of Obstetrics & Gynecology, USC School of Medicine, answers the question, How can I protect myself from getting sexually transmitted diseases? by saying, "Preventative measures include limiting sexual activity particularly to one uninfected partner. Other measures to reduce one's chances of sexually transmitted disease, *but not guaranteed,* include. . ."[2] S. I. McMillen concludes this topic with a point of view from his book, *None of These Diseases,* by saying, "Medical science with all its knowledge is inadequate to take care of the world's venereal disease problem. Yet millenniums before the microscope, and before man knew the method of the transmission of venereal diseases, God knew all about them and gave to man the only feasible plan of preventing these universal and blighting killers."[3]

7. Premarital sex hurts your walk with God.

When you have sex before marriage it causes you to stumble and fall. Your walk with God becomes strained to say the least. Your time alone with the Lord stops. You stop praying altogether. Pretty soon you're so far away from the Lord it feels as if you are all alone. You become unhappy and depressed. This I say because of experience. After I was divorced I started to go out with an old friend. We were very close. I was hurting and he was there, kind, gentle and reassuring. In the state I was in it wasn't hard to give in to sex with him. We had an ongoing relationship for quite some time. During that time I still went to church and so did he. I felt just like a hypocrite. I fell away from God. You can't have a relationship with Jesus when you are willfully sinning against Him!

8. **There can be resentment between marriage partners if one's virginity was lost before marriage and the other's wasn't.**

Also there was no resentment if both partners "saved" themselves for marriage. As an acquaintance once said to me, "Why did I keep my virginity before I got married when Russ lost his?"

9. **Premarital sex causes self-esteem to go down.**

Every teenager must wrestle with this issue. A teenager is not a child, nor is he an adult. He is just beginning to form ideas about who he is, of his own acceptability, normalcy, desirability. Sex is often used to gain acceptance, and for a moment he will find himself overwhelmingly accepted. But when he is left without emotional commitment, or love, the human spirit is punctured, and growth, maturity and self-acceptance spill out.

I was a casualty. I did not consent to my first
sexual relationship as a teenager, and perhaps this
has affected my viewpoint. But then a time came
when I did consent, due mostly to lowered self-esteem, loss of self-respect. I had lost my virginity, so
what was the fight for? I was ashamed before God,
and took a leave of absence from Him and my faith,
I think mostly because I could not forgive myself. I
wanted to be loved. I wanted to be cherished. My
father was gone; my heart was already torn into tiny
threads, threads I tried to wrap around a man. But
it was a dependent love. I needed it to survive.

I am whole now; I know God more intimately
now than ever before. When I was far from Him,
so was my peace.

10. A break-up after having premarital sex with a person will leave scars.

One issue that often comes up is that of long-term
boyfriend-girl friend relationships, the argument
being that sex is perfectly acceptable as long as the
two partners "love" each other and know what they
are getting into. This is not an exception to God's
law. This expression of love may seem to enhance
a relationship, but in the end will only cause much
more pain. Once a couple, having been involved in
sex, breaks up, both will feel as if they have lost
part of themselves. This is so because they have.
Breakup in this situation could even be compared
to the breakup of a marriage.

11. Premarital sex breaks down communication within the relationship.

Too early sexual involvement can blind a pair to
the other important aspects of their relationship that

they should be building as a sound foundation for their marriage. All too often they "fall into bed" rather than talk out the many things that should be shared and discussed. Once sexual intercourse starts, their interpersonal communication slackens off. Thus, in their coming together the couple may lose the very thing they sought to ensure — intimacy and companionship as a pair.

12. Premarital sex makes it more difficult to break up with someone.

Although having sex does tend to hurt a relationship, it also makes it harder for a couple to break up. Breaking up when you've had sex together can be a terribly emotionally tearing experience. Sex creates an emotional bond between people which is so powerful it's best reserved for marriage.

13. The desire for sex and not love becomes predominant.

I can remember two long-term relationships that I had that I knew would never amount to anything, but the excitement of sex made me a slave to pleasure. Like a drug, sex demanded heavier dosages to satisfy my desires. I began to use and exploit my girl friends rather than love them. Every time I attempted to break off these empty relationships, I was drawn back by the intense emotions that sex had created between the two of us.

14. Guilt can be avoided.

Another consequence of violating God's standard regarding sex before marriage is guilt. One of the worst feelings many sexually active people experience is waking up the next morning and realizing that the person lying next to them is a total stranger. This "morning after" syndrome begins to rob a person of a healthy self-image and a clear conscience, which decreases his ability to experience the transparency needed to cultivate an intimate relationship. On top of that, flashbacks from past sexual encounters can haunt a person the rest of his life which can leave him feeling "grimy" in the hands of his current lover. It's been said that "a good conscience is a continual good feast while a bad conscience is worse than a thousand enemies testifying against you."

15. Unwanted pregnancies and abortions can be prevented.

Next, take pregnancy. Abortion has made its resolve. But abortion never resolves the guilt, or breaks the bond between a mother and her baby.

Recently, I read these statistics by Dr. Anne Catherine Speckhard, Ph.D. of the University of Minnesota, on the long-term manifestations of stress from abortion 5 to 10 years later:

81 percent reported *preoccupation* with the aborted child.

73 percent reported *flashbacks* of the abortion experience.

69 percent reported feelings of *"craziness"* after the abortion.

54 percent recalled *nightmares* related to the abortion.

35 percent had perceived *visitations* from the aborted child.

23 percent reported *hallucinations* related to the abortion.

In Dr. Speckhard's findings, 72 percent of the subjects said they held no religious beliefs at the time of their abortion, and 96 percent in retrospect regarded abortion as the taking of life or as murder.[4]

16. There is only one "first time."

If you decide, that night, to be "with" this person while you are both unwed, you are essentially saying "my will be done." You're taking a very precious part of yourself and giving it to someone (who is more than willing to take it) who is not committed to you or the permanence of the relationship. This gift, once given, can never be taken back when you realize that you have made a mistake.

17. Waiting brings true fulfillment on the wedding night and in marriage.

Isn't it true that the things we save and work for are worth more to us? I can remember as a child working to save every nickel for a stereo. There were times my mother wanted to make up the allotted difference to help me purchase the stereo, but I wanted to do it all on my own. I'll never forget how special that day was when I could buy the gift for which I had long waited. It seems the stereo is even more valuable to me than what it is actually worth. I still have it, and have often considered selling it in a garage sale since it's old and outdated (how 'bout that 8-track?) but every time I listen to it I am reminded to persevere for the things that are worthwhile. The same holds true in waiting to have sex until after the marriage. It is easy to compromise and compensate for the time remaining until the wedding, but look ahead and think about the value of waiting. How much more special will the marriage be to the one who can hold out!

18. Fear of sexual comparison when married will be avoided.

There could also be a tendency to compare the sexual performance of one's spouse to previous sexual partners, especially if the "experienced" partner is left unsatisfied by his or her spouse. This has the potential to drive a wedge between the husband and wife, preventing them from experiencing God's desire for true intimacy and love expression in their marriage. The occurrence of mental flashbacks to an earlier sexual experience with a person other than one's mate is not unusual either. The flashback might happen during idle thinking time while walking down the street, or while trying to have a quiet time with the Lord, or in the passion of a sexual embrace with one's spouse. I know the frustration and disturbing effects of these flashbacks personally. I regret having had any kind of sexual involvement with anyone other than my wife, and wish I could completely erase these memories from my mind.

19. You will not be subject to God's judgment.

Hebrews 13:4 says: "Marriage should be honored by all, and the marriage bed be kept pure, for God will judge the adulterer and all the sexually immoral" (NIV). If this is true, and I believe it is, then how much more should the marriage bed be honored before one is married? Wouldn't we also be judged and punished by God for something this important? The Bible says we will reap what we sow. This would certainly apply to immoral acts.

20. Divorce rate among those who have premarital sex is high.

Some studies show that twice as many engagements are broken among couples who have had intercourse. Furthermore, they are more likely to be divorced or separated or to indulge in adultery. One way or another premarital intimacy is more closely connected to broken relationships than to solid ties.

21. Avoiding premarital sex builds trust in the marriage relationship.

Because people's feelings of love are strongly connected to the character of the loved one, a person's stand on premarital sex will affect his partner's emotions toward him. When a man (or woman) encourages his date to be involved sexually, he is teaching her about his character. She may excuse him at the time for his passion because of the love she feels, but the underlying message she has received is that he is morally weak in character and does not hold true to his conscience when tempted by passion. What results is that trust is destroyed, and trust is the foundation of any relationship on any level. The relationship in which there is little trust of moral character is never emotionally fulfilled.

22. Premarital sex hurts one's relationship with his or her parents.

It is there that I turn to my church and my family. When I lay next to my husband on our wedding night, I did not need to sneak away before dawn. My parents knew where we were. We had their blessing. The church had witnessed our vows before God. We had their blessing. Friends and family had sent cards of congratulations. It was right in "my crowd's" eyes as well as my Lord's. I had waited long for my wedding day and I have been enjoying that relationship ever since.

23. Waiting will bring God's blessing.

Waiting will give you the reward of God's blessing upon your life, because obedience to God always brings God's blessing. The book, *Be Challenged,* by Warren Wiersbe encourages teenagers to wait for God's best. "The tragedy is that too many young people are sacrificing their fantastic future for a fun-filled present. Today's toil is really a postponed pleasure. The real teenager is willing to let God prepare him for a fantastic future."[5]

24. Waiting produces dignity.

One reason God gives us His loving commands is that our *dignity* will be preserved. Dignity is the sense of nobility, worthiness and honor that God puts in every man. It is an understanding man has that for some reason man is more than just an animal. God, within His nature, has nobility and dignity. He has created man in His own image. Man's awareness of dignity results from his being created in the image of God.

25. Premarital sex often leads to extramarital sex.

Premarital sex can also harm one's future marriage. *Premarital Sex in a Changing Society* by Robert R. Bell explains that premarital sex increases the chance of extramarital sex which often leads to divorce. Still, some ask what the importance of the piece of paper is to marriage. Studies shown by *Family Life* magazine say that "intimacy produces more broken relationships than strengthened ones." Love can wait to give, but lust cannot wait to get.[6]

26. Jesus can fill the need for intimacy without sex.

Since becoming a Christian, I have realized that the spiritual emptiness I thought could only be filled by another person was only filled by Jesus Christ. And I can feel that same deep, intimate love without sex. I also see that because that union is so sacred, and you do become one with the person, God has reserved it for the sanctity of marriage. Sex is the greatest display of love possible next to dying for someone, to be shared by only those who have made the commitment to love each other for better or worse the rest of their lives. I am very grateful to be forgiven and released from my guilt, and to have a new beginning by being a virgin again in God's eyes, and to wait this time to share that intimacy only with my husband.

27. Premarital sex is a sin against your body.

I feel sex before marriage is not only "wrong," but in the Bible we are told this is also a sin against the body! In 1 Corinthians 6:16-20, a passage on sexual immorality, verse 18 says: "Flee [run away] from sexual immorality. All other sins a man commits are outside his body, but he who sins sexually sins against his own body" (NIV). This sin is the *only* one that is a sin against our bodies! (Believe me, there are repercussions suffered from willful disobedience. I went through a lot of unnecessary, gut-wrenching pain and heartbreak when I separated myself from the Lord.)

28. Premarital sex can lead to sexual addiction.

Now Crystal, a former drug dealer, spoke up. "Premarital sex is like drugs. You keep wanting bigger highs. In fact, I think it made me do more drugs, too. I'd get high, and then I'd do some weird, kinky stuff. Regular sex wasn't enough. I'd do things I felt horrible about. Then I'd do more drugs to take away the pain. It was a vicious circle."

29. Don't cause a weaker brother to sin.

Christians have the responsibility of making sure they are not causing a weaker Christian to sin. If a Christian is heard to have had premarital sex, another Christian may easily be influenced as to what he (or she) will do when he has a choice to make about premarital sex.

30. It is a poor testimony for Christ.

First, as Christians we are a witness to many non-Christians during our lifetime. As we go through life we need to remember that our actions will always speak louder than our words. I feel that premarital sex is a very "loud" action, therefore it would not be good for our testimony as a Christian.

31. Waiting shows your marriage partner how much you love him or her.

There is one more reason I say a person should wait for marriage to engage in sex. On July 27, 1985, God gave me the most wonderful man in the world to be my husband. I asked for Prince Charming, and He gave me *much more* than that. He gave me someone I can share my deepest feeling with, someone I can talk to God with, someone I know will always love me and be faithful to me, and most of all, someone I am *so* glad I waited for. I thank God for him. And on our wedding night, I experienced my first time (of sex) with my husband. I wouldn't have wanted to share my first time with *anyone* else. I had no riches or jewels to offer my husband, but he wanted no riches or jewels. All he wanted was me . . . and I sure had that to give to him — *all* of me and my body, untouched and *his alone.* This was a good enough reason for me to wait.

32. Premarital sex can give rise to misleading feelings.

Looking back, I think you will realize how you thought that you were in control of your life by seeing the fulfillment of what you desired come to pass, that is "living fast and loose" with no thought of anyone but yourself. This seems to be more of a "selfish-control" rather than self-control, and has led you to the other side of life as a result of your actions. Now there is only depression over your experiences, and a feeling of emptiness. At the age of 15, you professed your belief in the salvation of Jesus Christ; and now at 17, you feel lost and empty, and want to die.

33. Once you engage in premarital sex, it is easier to do it again.

Even if a person has gotten away from all sexually involved relationships and has tried to work through the guilt and anger, there still remain consequences.

Any sin has consequences, and premarital sex involves some of the most far-reaching consequences of all. Dating becomes more difficult due to a constant underlying fear of falling back into sexual involvement again. Premarital sex opens Pandora's box to an entire area that should never have been experienced before marriage. It is always easier to do something the second time around, and once a person has become active sexually, he simply does not forget.

34. Premarital sex buries love.

The development of a relationship can be inhibited because much of a couple's time together will become dominated by sex. A couple can tend to stop investing energy into exploring the many facets of each other's personalities that deepen relationships. The curiosity is gone and so is the mystery. It's easy for boredom to set in.

Love is hurt in a relationship where sex is explored outside of marriage. It can cause future sexual problems in the marriage. Trobisch illustrates this idea in this way: "Premarital sex is rather like picking blossoms in spring. It seems beautiful, right and natural. But when autumn comes, there is no fruit."

35. Waiting brings maturity.

People should wait until marriage to engage in sex because waiting gives your mind and body the time it needs to mature.

36. Expectations fail.

If I could give any reason as my most persuasive, it would be this one. Many have given in to passion as I did, in the heat of the moment. I have heard many say they regretted this. Others have waited until they were married. I have yet to hear *one* of *them* say they are sorry.

37. Premarital sex induces performance syndrome.

Sexually active people also suffer from comparison and the performance syndrome. Debora Phillips, author of *Sexual Confidence* and director of Princeton Center for Behavior Therapy in New Jersey, states that "due to the instant sex of the sexual revolution, people perform rather than make love. Many women can't achieve a sense of intimacy, and their anxiety about how well they perform blocks their chances for honest arousal. Without genuine involvement, they haven't much chance for courtship, romance or love. They're left feeling cheated and burned out."[7]

38. Bad memories of broken friendships stay with you.

Is it possible to share physical intimacy with a boyfriend/girl friend and upon breaking up be able to say goodbye physically and emotionally? This writer's experience says no. The act of sexual intercourse is bonding, not just physically, but emotionally and spiritually as well. If I would have had a healthy relationship (without sexual involvement), I know the road to recovery from a breakup would have been shortened and the heartbreak would have been minor in comparison. Instead, the recovery was long because the attachment was strong. I had given a part of myself away and the memories were my reminder. How can the imagery of oneness be erased? It's been painful and difficult to train my mind to "think on whatever is right and pure and lovely" (see Philippians 4:8).

39. Waiting brings real freedom.

How can waiting until marriage before experiencing sexual relationships really mean freedom? In our day and age? Everyone knows that freedom means doing whatever I want, with whomever I want, whenever I want. Right? Not necessarily. Real freedom is not just doing anything with anyone at anytime. If everyone did that, it would not be freedom; it would be chaos. Real freedom can be expressed through the following illustration by Sir Rabindranath Tagore: "I have on my table a violin string. It is free. I twist one end of it and it responds. It is free. But it is not free to do what a violin string is supposed to do — to produce music. So I take it, fix it in my violin and tighten it until it is taut. Only then is it free to be a violin string."[8]

Real freedom comes when the thing created is free to perform the function for which it was created. In the area of sexual relationships, total freedom comes when sex is left to the confines of marriage. Like the violin string that performs its intended function, sexual pleasure produces the sweetest music within the limits of married love.

40. It's a sin against God.

We were high school sweethearts. She was a pom-pon girl. I was a jock. It only seemed natural that many of our dates would end up in the back seat of my car, "the bomb," at 2 A.M.

We were both virgins prior to that "first time." She was 17 and I was 18. I assured her that I loved her, told her that contraceptives were not needed and convinced her that our relationship could withstand even an unwanted pregnancy. My dad's stern command, "Just keep your pants zipped," rang loud and clear in my mind, but I thoroughly enjoyed my freedom to disobey him. I had conformed to his wishes long enough.

That first time was all it took. As our sexual contact increased, our relationship slowly diminished. I went 400 miles away to college, convinced that our relationship could withstand the separation, but it didn't. She saw other guys, and I broke two knuckles by furiously punching a cement wall in the dorm when I found out. That was the end, I thought.

We found our way back together the summer before my junior year. The back of the car became familiar again. After school started in the fall, she came down to visit me. Determined never to lose her again, I asked her that weekend to marry me, and we celebrated in the dorm bed. Again we used no contraceptives, and this time she became pregnant.

We rushed into a December wedding, and with the help of many others, I managed to finish school. Now, seven years later, we have become Christians, have three great kids, and are seeking to please God daily. Our premarital sex resulted in marriage, new lives in Christ and three beautiful children! Should I regret my premarital encounters? Even though much good has come after premarital sex, I must admit that I really do regret it. Let me explain.

There are three main reasons why I agree with any father who tells his son to "keep your pants zipped" until marriage. First, premarital sex is a sin that God abhors. No matter how good it feels, no matter how long you've waited, no matter what your peers tell you, the fact remains: Premarital sex is sin. Genesis 2:18-25 explains God's three-step plan for marriage: (1) Leave the child relationship with your parents; (2) then cleave, or totally commit yourself to your mate, now and for the future; and then finally (3) become one flesh sexually, mentally and spiritually in service to God. Marriage out of this three-step sequence is not God's plan. And being anywhere outside God's plan is sin.

In our relationship, we had committed to a physical relationship before committing ourselves totally to each other and God's purpose for us. Although we did not know God at the time, that gave us no reason to break His commands for the marriage sequence. My dad was not a Christian at the time either, but his command was morally in line with God. In fact, down deep, I knew it was wrong, but I justified it by deceiving myself and my girl friend.

41. Premarital sex can make it difficult to make proper decisions regarding the relationship.

Another pertinent reason to refrain from premarital sex is that a sexual relationship outside of marriage tends to portray a false sense of intimacy to those gripped in its tentacles. Feelings of lust and infatuation can easily be mistaken for "true love." This surface (physical) love, joined with the resulting emotional attachment, can lead to a premature marriage, which in turn could end up in divorce if the couple is unprepared to face and cope with the reality of everyday practicality and the relational conflict that does occur in marriage. The same situation could apply for two people who are actively seeking to know whether or not they may be "right" for each other. In this case, their sexual relationship could prevent them from seeing themselves and their relationship clearly, much like a cloud that prevents the rays of the sun from shining its light on the earth below. Their sexual involvement clouds the picture of what direction the relationship should take, making it extremely difficult to discern what the best decision is regarding their future together. Again the commands of Scripture and God's guidelines concerning premarital sex are truly for our own benefit and welfare.

42. Waiting for marriage can lead to good habit patterns.

Picture a pair of lovers atop a moonlit hillside covered with fresh, sparkling snow. Surely it is a scene for romance. Imagine a sled cutting its path through the snow for the first time as it slides down the hillside. Again and again the sled packs its path, making snowy banks on either side that eventually become barriers which force the sled to follow its original pattern. It is the same with the lovers. As they enter a sexual relationship with each other, they are cutting a path which, when repeated, becomes the pattern their sex lives have a strong tendency to follow for the rest of their lives. How important it is to make the first path a good one.

43. Premarital sex can have bad effects on children.

Perhaps the most tragic result of premarital sex is the children that result. Often these children are unwanted, and consequently neglected and abused. The children may grow up in a one-parent home of a young mother who is herself a child and not mentally or emotionally ready to raise a child. (Also, she may not be financially stable.) Who suffers? The young mother, the child, and the families involved. The children that result from premarital sexual acts (if not aborted) face life with the odds against them. Unlike children in two-parent homes, where the adults are likely to be more mature both mentally and emotionally to raise their children, the single-parent child is missing a role model to learn from.

44. Waiting keeps respect for each other.

I was out the other night with Heather and it was really tempting for me; we were all alone at her house because her parents went out for a while. I am really glad that nothing happened because it would have ruined everything between us. We have a great time together without sex getting involved. I feel that it's just not the right time to get sexually involved with her; there's too much to lose. We might have lost the respect that we always had for each other, and we'd lose the things that keep us close.

45. Premarital sex may hurt your reputation.

The young teenage years are a time when one's reputation is severely judged by one's peers. When a girl engages in premarital sex, every boy in that school district will now know what kind of girl she is. This applies to older women in an employment situation. When at the job, people tend to boast about their sexual conquests, and you may be the subject of their stories because of your indiscretion.

46. God has our best interests in mind.

God's views on premarital sex and its conflicts can be found by reading His Word. God knows what is best for us. Therefore, when He commands us not to fornicate, it is for our own benefit to obey Him.

In the parent-child relationship, we are taught this principle. When a parent commands a child not to run into the street when a car is coming, it is for his own safety. We have to believe the parent as our authority on this subject because they know what is best for us. We have to trust our parent on this. We are not going to run into the street before an oncoming car just to see if what they said is true. God is our all-knowing Father who has the right to guide us in how we live our lives.

47. Premarital sex can lead to bad consequences for the entire society.

Society — even those who choose to remain pure from sexual immorality — will partially bear the burden of venereal disease, unwanted pregnancies, and broken relationships. Collectively, we as a covenant nation have chosen to condone premarital sex and are now reaping its wicked fruits.

25

37 Ways to Say No

The following thirty-seven ways to say no to premarital sex were suggested by the teens themselves.

1. Go to the Creator who created us, who knows how we run best.

First of all, God created the world and everything which exists within the world. As creator and sustainer God has the patent on His invention. If I invent an automobile that rivals every car that has been invented heretofore, I have the right to patent that automobile. It is my creation. If I want to change or modify anything in my design, by law I have that right. Let's say that I marketed that unusual vehicle and you bought one. If that car broke down, would you feel more comfortable taking it to "Bill's Gas Station" for repairs or to my service center? Of course you would feel more comfortable bringing it to my service center because I built it and would know before anyone else what is best for the car. "Return to the manufacturer for repair."

2. Control your own body.

I know that premarital sex is *not* one of His desires for any of His children's lives. In 1 Thessalonians 4:3,4,7,8, Paul, Silas, and Timothy write: "It is God's will that you should . . . avoid sexual immorality; that each of you should learn to control his own body in a way that is holy and honorable. . . . For God did not call us to be impure, but to live a holy life. Therefore, he who rejects this instruction does not reject man but God"(NIV).

3. Build a relationship with Jesus so that your loneliness will be satisfied.

It's important to stay in a close relationship with Jesus. My boyfriend and I have discovered that if we start drifting away from Jesus, we are more vulnerable to our sexual feelings. If your relationship with God is not right, then no other relationship can be right either. If both of you are right with God, then it is so much easier to go to Him when you need assistance.

4. Develop a set of convictions.

Convictions are the things that make people rise to the top. What the business field calls the "cream of the crop" in speaking of C.E.O.s are the ones who have simply risen to the top. You do know that cream always rises to the top, don't you? Well, now you know how they got there. It wasn't by chance that the climber found himself at the top of Mt. Everest one day. It took great convictions, careful planning, and knowing what to avoid.

May I submit to you that that's exactly how life is, too? It's true. And the thing I would like to come from both your and my life during these early years is a set of convictions that will cause us to be different, to rise to the top, to be a light to the world around us, a set of convictions that we could and would die for.

It's my belief that at the top of that list should be the conviction of where our dating and sex life is going to go, when it's going to go, and how far it's going to go. If we were simply to allow ourselves to drift in this particular area of our lives, we would be no different from the rest of our sick and dying world.

5. Learn to say "no."

I know a lot of people who have had premarital sex because of peer pressure, and I think it is really sad. But that is what I almost made the mistake of doing. Today's society is getting so bold. I think, though, that if you don't let down to going to bed with a guy, telling him no, later on down the line he will tell you that he respects you for saying no, and that he wishes the other girls would have said no. He says that he was either mad at someone, and wanted to get back at them, or that he was just plain being rebellious. I've had this happen. The day after, or maybe even a week, or sometimes longer, he will tell you that he respects and looks up to you for saying no!

6. Take preventative measures to avoid temptations.

You don't have to have sex before marriage. Your virginity is one of the most precious things that you possess, so guard it! You can throw it away like some worthless garbage, or you can save it like a priceless jewel. It's your choice. If you have trouble resisting temptation in your dating life, then avoid things that arouse the physical desires. Don't go into dark places by yourselves. Don't spend too much time alone in the car. Don't always feel you have to single-date. Don't listen to music and don't watch movies that feed the flesh.

7. Repent and walk in God's grace and His provisions.

Confess your sin to God for the Bible has no limit on forgiveness. But Jesus says also that you must change. The main dividing line in God's eye is between those who are children of God and those who are not. God's children aren't marked by a history of never doing anything wrong, instead they are marked as those who have accepted God's forgiveness and committed themselves to following Him. Take the attitude that Jesus showed in John 8:11, "Neither do I condemn you. . . . Go now and leave your life of sin" (NIV).

8. Meditate on God's Word to be "transformed by the renewing of your mind."

First of all, you must meditate on the Word. This is work. I don't just mean read a chapter a day and go on your merry way, telling yourself that "greater is He that is in you than he that is in the world." That's true, but how long does it take you to read that chapter? Ten minutes, max? And that leaves the rest of the day to be bombarded by the lies of the world, the devil, and even your own flesh. Sure, God is greater, but with that kind of "commitment," He may not think you're too serious about wanting His help. MEDITATE. That means memorize and think about — analyze, consider, ponder, even question (with a heart willing to accept true answers) pertinent Scriptures. Say with the psalmist, "Thy Word I have treasured in my heart, that I may not sin against Thee" (Psalm 119:11, NASB).

9. Seek godly counsel.

Find someone you will have to answer to often, perhaps weekly. Knowing we'll have to confess that sin to someone whose love and respect is important to us can really help.

10. Flee or break up.

When you try to point out that the Bible says premarital sex is wrong, the common reaction is: "They didn't have the same kinds of temptations we do today." This is a cop-out, because in Genesis 39:7-12 we are told the story of Joseph being tempted by Potiphar's wife. Potiphar's wife was absolutely infatuated with Joseph. She tried her best to seduce him, saying, "Lie with me." Now Joseph was left in charge of the entire household while Potiphar was away on business. There was no one there to catch them, and Potiphar's wife was very beautiful. But Joseph was smart, and verse 10 says: "Joseph day by day . . . hearkened not unto her, to lie by her, or to be with her" (KJV). I suppose Joseph thought that if he wasn't around her, he wouldn't be as tempted. We can run from temptation the same way Joseph did.

It's true that there are more temptations today, but we haven't changed. We are the same and our desires are the same. You may be thinking, *Well, how can I get out of this way of thinking and acting?* God has provided a way to "kick the habit," a way

to avoid and deal with these temptations. In 1 Corinthians 10:13 it says: "There hath no temptation taken
you but such as is common to man: but God is
faithful, who will not suffer you to be tempted above
that ye are able; but will with the temptation also
make a way to escape, that ye may be able to bear
it" (KJV). You are not the only one in the world
facing sexual temptation. God is still on your side —
He has provided ways of escape. His ways of escape
are mostly before you enter the temptation. You can
do what Joseph did, not hang around the person
you are magnetically drawn to. Avoid that person,
and you won't be as tempted.

**11. Don't watch TV or movies that have sexually
based material.**

Stay away from pornography, magazines, movies,
TV, or anything else that stimulates you sexually.
Don't buy into the Hollywood line that life is a
constant romance seeking sexual satisfaction. Reject
the concept that the other person is there to fulfill
your expectations. People are not to be manipulated,
either for sexual satisfaction or for security in marriage. Learn to trust God for both. The bottom line
is don't let anybody or anything, including yourself,
convince you that sex is the best or only highway
to greater happiness and fulfillment in life.

**12. "Take captive every thought to make it obe-
dient to Christ" (2 Corinthians 10:5, NIV).
Don't let your mind dwell on the wrong
things (fantasies, sexual scenes, etc.).**

Sinful action starts with sinful thought. Have you
ever noticed how often the Bible refers to keeping
our minds pure? Jesus tells us that if a man looks

on a woman with lust, he has already committed adultery with her in his heart. In other words, the thought is as bad as the deed. Therefore, any activity that leads you to lust after another person is wrong. When you lust after someone, you begin to view them as an object rather than as a person, and this viewpoint will eventually be evidenced in your actions.

13. Stop dating and get your thoughts straight.

Pat first had sex when she was sixteen. She became a Christian the next year and although she eventually learned that sex outside of marriage was wrong, she was often frustrated by her inability to break an established habit pattern of exchanging sex for "love." Finally Pat decided to stop dating for a couple of years so she could get her thoughts together. It was a time of incredible spiritual growth and it seemed that God was giving her victory in an area that had been a "thorn in the flesh" for so long!

14. Avoid the "little sins"; they lead to big ones.

Sin often starts small and grows to unmanageable proportions. It's easy to disregard what seems like a "little sin," an impure thought or slightly impure action. Remember that once we start excusing sin it becomes easier and easier to excuse larger and larger sins. Also remember that lust has an insatiable appetite; the more you feed it, the hungrier it gets.

15. Communicate with each other your feelings about sexual involvement.

Talk honestly with Mike about your feelings toward sexual involvement. Try to describe your feelings in as many ways as possible and keep talking to him (perhaps on several different occasions) until *you* are sure he understands what you are saying. Use "I" statements and appeal to his desires. Here are some examples that may help you:

(a) I don't like the spiritual side effects that erode my relationship with God and make me more irritable with you.

(b) I feel like I begin to lose respect and admiration for you and I'll need those things if I'm going to learn how to be a submissive wife.

(c) I feel like I'm being conditioned to reach a certain level of sexual excitement at which point I have to "turn myself off" and I'm afraid that will keep me from giving myself to you fully in bed once we are married.

(d) I feel like I'm learning to associate sex with furtiveness, shame and secrecy rather than with the love, trust and openness that we want to characterize our married sex life.

16. Make yourselves accountable.

Make yourself accountable if you have continued problems. Share your problem with an older Christian woman and ask Mike to talk to an older man. Knowing that you'll have to answer to someone outside of yourselves is a powerful deterrent.

17. Sit down and write out some goals of what you want for your relationship and your convictions.

What do you say we get together next week and make a list — together, I mean — of the things we would really like to see accomplished in our lives? Then we'll also make a note of the price we're going to have to pay to see them come true. I think we could be great accountability partners for each other, don't you? I think we need each other. Let's help each other climb out of the pits of mediocrity and be all that God created us to be. I think we can make it to the top!

18. Ask God to help you.

The next step is to pray together. Admit to God that you need His help in conquering your sexual desires. Prayer is one of the biggest helps there is. Also, both need to pray about this problem privately.

19. Build a "Christian conscience."

Doing this will pay off, because if you let your sense of right and wrong be your guide, you'll be giving yourself the gift of self-respect. And self-respect is as precious as your right to say no.

20. Hang around people who have the same values you have.

In 1 Corinthians 5:9 it says: "I wrote you in my letter not to associate with immoral people" (NASB). When you hang around and associate with immoral people you become immoral yourself. Why is this? Because if everyone is having premarital sex and talking about it, your conscience becomes salved and you no longer feel the conviction against it. In fact, your friends would encourage it. You would begin to feel the pressure after so long. The girls would make you feel that you weren't very attractive and you weren't worth much, and the guys would make you feel like a wimp and not experienced like other girls. After so much of that from the crowd that you are with, you say, what the heck, and do it! Even so you know it is wrong, but peer pressure overrules! At that point you lay down all your morals and turn your back on God's commandments.

21. Commit each date to the Lord; be Christ-like, and act like Jesus would if He were on a date.

To stay out of such a "sex trap" one must first commit all his dating relationships to the Lord. He is to be Christ-like, and act like Jesus would if He were on a date. He should also look at his girl friend or date as the Lord does — at her inward character, not her outward appearance (1 Samuel 16:7). If he really loves his girl friend, he should not have to "prove" it to her through sex, but it should be evident in the way he treats her daily through kindness, patience, unselfishness and forgiveness. If your motive in relationships is to please and bring glory to God, and you practice it, I am sure that God will bless you with many great relationships!

22. Realize that God has a special purpose for your life.

Know that there is a God in heaven who cares for you very much. He has designed you and your sexuality for a specific plan in your life — to take place in the context of marriage.

23. Don't think that you are strong enough to "handle it" when the temptation comes.

In our society today, the temptation to have premarital sex is so strong, especially among the younger generation. Young people find themselves in situations that they can't say no to. For it may have seemed right at the time, but the after-effect made it seem so wrong. So many times we say, "Oh, I can handle it if I'm ever in that situation." They don't decide before going in; instead they try to stop in the middle. It's like reading a good book — once you've started it, it's hard to stop.

24. Realize that there is nothing wrong with sex in the proper situation. It is what God has planned.

Rick, you have lived near me for nearly five months and know that I will respond from a biblical perspective. The fact is that your desire for an intimate relationship with a woman, and even your desire for sex, is not wrong or sinful. In fact, in Genesis 2:18-25, God demonstrated to Adam his need for a helper and then created woman to be his wife. One entire book of the Bible, the Song of Solomon, is a story of two lovers speaking to each other. In Ephesians, chapter 5, the apostle Paul describes the relationship between a husband and wife and summarizes it in verse 32: "I am speaking with reference to Christ and the Church" (NASB). In other words, God gave to man the desire for an intimate relationship through sex and esteems this relationship so highly that Jesus is called the Groom, and the corporate body of believers — the Church — shall be united with Jesus as His Bride (Revelation 19:7-9).

25. Plan your dates; be creative. Occupy yourselves with other activities.

Kids often say, "What else is there to do?" If we want to wait until marriage to have sex, we need to plan dates. Be creative, do something fun and silly. Play games like Trivial Pursuit, Monopoly, Parcheesi and others. If it's a nice day, play volleyball or softball, or swim. Something different to do would be to rent a video camera and make movies or commercials. Use your imagination to really "have fun" and stay chaste.

26. Set your standards before the relationship starts.

Set your standards NOW, not when you're deep into a relationship, for what you will allow in a relationship. Set them according to what is right in the eyes of God. Keep your morals clean and high. Don't lower them for anyone. For those who have a hard time getting dates, their morals tend to lower and lower until it gets them into a situation they can't get out of.

27. Don't assume that you have gone too far or sinned too much for God to be able to redeem you both and help you find fulfillment in each other.

I love you and I want to see you repair your relationship with God.

You may be feeling very guilty now. That's because real guilt is caused by real sin and needs to have real forgiveness. You may feel that God doesn't love you or won't forgive what you've done because He feels so strongly against it. But I can tell you that there is nothing that you could ever do to keep God from loving you or to make Him stop. His love is unconditional and no matter what you do, God is always standing there with open arms, ready to receive you when you turn back to Him. He longs to have you back with Him. He wants to take your sins and throw them into the depths of the seas. And as Corrie Ten Boom adds, He puts up a "No Fishing" sign.

28. Consider the benefits you would have by waiting to have sex until after marriage.

So many teenagers feel that God is trying to cheat them by telling them that it is wrong to have sex before marriage. It's just the opposite! God wants only the absolute best for you! Girls, what guy wants someone who has been fondled and touched like a once beautiful rose? Guys, what girl wants someone who has been with every other girl in town? God wants you to have someone who is totally yours, someone who has saved himself (or herself) just for you, someone you can learn with, someone who has never touched anyone the way he has touched you. He wants you to have someone who truly loves you, not someone who loves your body. True love is not selfish.

29. Be involved in a group where you can be real and can gain support.

I have never engaged in premarital sex in my relationships. I am neither proud nor ashamed of the fact because it is largely due to my Christian upbringing. Throughout my adolescence and college years I had a strong network of friends and fellow church members who provided the support and caring needed through those unsure times. The care and intimacy derived from these special people has given me enough security and love to save the act of sexual intercourse for the person I choose to become one with.

30. When a person who is tempting comes around, start talking about Jesus Christ.

The most effective way I have found to say no is to start talking about Jesus Christ. If that won't convict you, I don't know what will.

The first time I tried doing this I was at work and this guy was trying to pick up on me, and I knew the only reason he was asking me out was to get me in bed. He asked for my phone number and I gave it to him. Then I invited him to Skyline Collegians for our first date, but that didn't go over so well. Within five minutes of that he was telling me what a nice girl I was and handing me my phone number back. Like they say, if you've never tasted candy, you won't miss it.

31. Do not become too committed to the "steady" relationship too quickly, but in the proper timing.

Maturity and being responsible can determine if you are ready to date. If you date before you are ready, you will have a lot of problems. When you date before you are ready, sometimes you let your emotions get in the way and you cannot control them. Then the guy or girl can easily persuade you to have sex. Do not let a guy or girl persuade you or pressure you into doing what you know is wrong. Love can wait, but lust cannot. The Bible says in 1 Corinthians 5:11 to stay away from fornicators.

32. Let your words and actions be proper so that those who want sex will avoid you because they know where you stand.

If somebody desires physical contact, that person will search for a date with someone who has proliferated sex, by either verbal or visual means. On the other hand, a person who is known to be respectful of others and their bodies will be ignored by this individual. The bottom line is that we are all judged on the basis of our words and our actions, and by this representation, others will seek what they want. Because I have been outspoken about my beliefs, those who would be inclined to have premarital sex avoid me and I avoid them. That takes some pressure off me and makes a good working relationship.

33. Date only those who have convictions similar to yours.

If a guy or girl pressures you, then you should not see him or her any more. The Bible says in Ecclesiastes 3:3 that there is "a time to tear down, and a time to build" (NIV). If he or she pulls you down instead of building or lifting you up, then you need not see him or her any more.

Some kids are dared by their friends. In Proverbs 17:17 the Bible says: "A friend loveth at all times"

(KJV). If your friends dare you or threaten or pressure you, then you do not need them. We should have enough respect and pride for ourselves that we would not give in to a dare just to be accepted. The Bible says in Proverbs 18:24: "A man that hath friends must shew himself friendly: and there is a friend that sticketh closer than a brother" (KJV). If our friends cannot accept us as we are, then they do not love us and we do not need them.

34. Never give up.

My final advice to you, Kelly, is to *never* give up. If you and Mike fall, remember that "love covers a multitude of sins." Forgive, forget, and move on, but don't give up hope for change. Pat made her fatal mistake when she decided that she didn't care any more and she started rationalizing her sin. Her heart soon became so hardened that she had no desire to change. Please, *please* don't let that happen to you.

35. Avoid being alone with each other.

Being in the dark and/or being someplace with no fear of interruption for a long period of time are plainly things to avoid. Proverbs 6:27,28 says that if you play with the fires of passion, you are going to get burned.

36. Have minimal physical contact.

After God healed my broken heart, I dated a very committed Christian for two years. His life radiated Christ and had such an impact on mine. The friendship was super and there was minimal physical contact.

37. Make a commitment before God.

I challenge you to give God a chance to work in your relationship. Make a commitment to Him to stop being sexually involved, and to wait for the right time with the right person. If you and your girl friend really are in love, then your love for each other will only grow stronger and deeper as you build your relationship on the Lord and save sex for its proper context. If your relationship just doesn't survive without the physical part, then it obviously wasn't right and God's best for you, and why settle for anything less than the best?

SECTION IV
Essays:
Writing Their Hearts Out

The Stain That Will Never Come Out

♥

A teenager reflects back to the age of thirteen and the trauma of being forced to face the decision of "showing your love" to an older boy. This is not an isolated struggle. It is a constant reality to the majority of teens.

She was extremely young, but she didn't feel young. It seemed like such a mature jump — from the young, immature age of twelve to the much more exciting, official teenager age of thirteen. She really loved being and "acting" older. She thought everything was great! She worked hard in school. She was an honor student and was also very involved in extra-curricular activities. She loved to do things, and to share deep, dark secrets with her best friend. She had a good family and her parents taught her well the difference between right and wrong. She was sensible and had a good head on her shoulders — so it seemed.

He was older than she and extremely popular. He was very talented and was always the center of attention. She was so overwhelmed with joy when he started to pay very special attention to her. She was so very pleased when he picked her to have as a girl friend rather than any of the other girls — who would have died for the chance.

One day he told her, "I love you." But she had nothing to say in return. She did not love him, yet adored the popularity he gained for her. She was blinded by the new attention she received, by her newly discovered "popularity." Everyone said "Hi" to her, everyone knew her. Everyone wanted to know her.

He asked her if he could express his love to her. She said she wasn't ready. He said, "I love you." She did not reply. Later, he told her something had happened. He said he showed his "love" to someone else, yet did not really love that someone else. She said it was all right. He said, "I love you." She looked down and said nothing.

She had never had so many friends before. So many people wanted to talk with her. In fact, she noticed that boys were paying a lot more attention to her. But she stayed with him . . . because he loved her.

Then he told her it happened again. He said he showed "love" to someone else, yet he did not really love that someone else. He even showed her who the girl was. She looked away. She felt threatened. But her told her, "I love you." She looked down and quietly replied the same.

He reacted. He told her to show her love for him. She didn't want to but she didn't want to lose him to someone else. So she showed her "love." He wanted to "love" her more, but this time she was definitely sure. She said, "No!"

She was very alone. She was violated. She was naive. She was innocent no longer. She broke up with him. He asked her to take him back. He told her, "I love you." But she rejected him. A few days later, he was in"love" with someone else.

She was impure and unwholesome. She was used. She was drowned in shame. She was swallowed up by guilt. Now she is afraid to ever love again. She is afraid to ever be loved again. She knows she can never change the past. She has stained her life . . . a stain that will never come out. She was extremely young. She finally realized how young.

The story is taken directly out of reality. Those are actual feelings of guilt, self-pity, hatred, shame and impurity that she felt at the young age of thirteen. In fact, some of those feelings still exist . . . I still feel them to this very day.

Having premarital sex was the most horrifying experience of my life. It wasn't at all the emotionally satisfying or the casually taken experience the world declares it to be. Having sex was extremely personal. I felt as if my insides were being exposed and my heart left unattended.

Sex is supposed to be an expression of love. The world's view of sex has been so distorted. The media has a strong influence on people's lives. And the media has been projecting that sex is love and love is having sex.

The media also has projected that sex can be something very casual. But God tells us not to be deceived (1 Corinthians 6:9) or conformed to the world (Romans 12:2). Sex is definitely something that God intended as an expression of love within marriage. If two people love each other enough to want to have sex, that means that they love each other enough to have a lifelong, committed relationship together. It means loving each other enough to be very intimate and personal with each other and no one else. It is a type of love that is unconditional and cherished. It is love that is not only run on emotions but also on real commitment. Sex is so deeply personal that it is the innermost expression of love that you would want to express only to a mate that you are positively sure you have a lifetime relationship with. Sex is something you want to give to only one person, within your marriage, because marriage is a very special and exclusive relationship (Hebrews 13:4).

Having premarital sex was the worst mistake I ever made. I shared myself with someone I didn't love and in my farthest thoughts never intended to marry. I exposed myself to someone who seemed as if he was a stranger because sex is so private. I know God has forgiven me of this haunting sin but I also know for a fact that I can never have my virginity back. Though God has completely forgotten, I cannot erase the past or ignore my future. Some day I will marry someone and share something very special with him, but I will also have to tell him of my sickening experience. I dread the day that I have to tell the man I truly love that he is not the only one, though I wish that he was.

♡ ♡ ♡

In Search of
My Father's Love

♥

A 27-year-old single woman looks at her present frustration with love and at her quest in the past for love and acceptance that could only be found in her "father's love."

A girl's sexual identity is defined by her father. A little girl grows up seeking her self-esteem — who she is — in her father and how he relates to her. If she has a father who loves her unconditionally, then she sees herself as a loved, secure, satisfied person and will have a good self-image.

If, however, she doubts her father's love and acceptance of her, she will seek that love elsewhere, not realizing that it's her daddy's love she is looking for. So, when the first boy comes along who claims he loves her, she will do almost anything to secure his love.

When I was only fourteen years of age, I dated an eighteen-year-old boy. After a month or so of dating, he told me that he loved me and had to "have me." He said that if I loved him, I would have sex with him. And if I wouldn't, he couldn't control his desire for me, and would have to break up with me.

What did I think at fourteen years of age? I knew sex was wrong before marriage, yet I so desired to have a man love me. I was so insecure in my father's love and had a poor self-image. I always felt like I had to *earn* people's love. The better I was at home with my chores, the more my father loved me, or so it was communicated. The more *A*'s on my report card, the more my father loved me. So here was my boyfriend, who I really liked, and thought I loved, telling me he loved me. Well, I needed that love. And if the conditions to keep that love were to have sex with him, I felt I had no choice. I didn't want to lose my virginity, but I also didn't want to lose the man who loved me. So I finally gave in.

I felt so guilty afterward. I can remember sobbing in my bed at nights, after I'd come home from being with my boyfriend. I wanted so much to have my virginity back. And yet it was gone, forever. My self-esteem certainly didn't improve, but worsened, and I needed my boyfriend's love more than ever. I began to feel so lonely inside, and yet there was no one I could turn to. Certainly not my father, who would really "hate" me if he ever knew what an awful thing I had done.

Well, after two years, I broke up with my boyfriend, but soon had another, and went through the same cycle with him. And then with another. Was I any more secure with myself? No, I was a puppet in any man's hands, for I wanted so desperately to find someone who would love me unconditionally.

Isn't that ironic? The very thing I searched for — unconditional love — was being offered to me conditionally . . . "If you love me, you'll do it."

At the age of twenty-one, I found that unconditional love. Jesus Christ. He loved me while I was a sinner, and died for my sins on the cross so that I could be His child and He could be my Father. He accepted me just the way I was.

I'm twenty-seven now, and about six months ago I wrote in my journal to the Lord these very words:

"I felt lonely tonight. And I thought about the many times in my life that I have felt lonely, intense loneliness. As though I were here in life all alone. And I realized that what I was lonely for was a 'daddy.' To be able to call him up when I hurt and hear him say he understands and have him listen to me. And I could call him because of our special relationship as I grew up.

"But I never had that with my dad. And so I am lonely without that link to my past. Yet tonight, God again spoke to me, in that still, quiet way, and said He was there for me. And as the tears poured, I said, 'Will You be my Daddy? Will You be there to talk to, just to talk to, and will You listen? Yes, I know You will. And the most wonderful thing about You as my Daddy is that I can be with You all the time. I'll never be without You, or Your love for me.'

"And then I thought about the young girl who this very night will lose her virginity because she is searching for love — her daddy's love. And I wanted to be able to stop her somehow and tell her that she'll never find it in another man. How my heart is wrenched when I think of this girl . . . when I think of myself, so many years ago. And my life has been a search for my daddy's love. And in Jesus, I am found and I am loved. Forever." August 11, 1985.

So what do I want parents to know about their child's sexuality? Children's sexuality is directly related to how they think of themselves. If they don't find the love that they need at home, they'll go looking for it elsewhere, but it will always be a cheap substitute for what a real daddy's love could be.

There's a song out by Steve and Annie Chapman which says:

Daddy you're the man in your little girl's dreams,
    you are the one she longs to please.
And there's a place in her heart
    that can only be filled
    with her daddy's love.
But if you don't give her the love she desires,
    she'll try someone else,
    but they won't satisfy'er.
And if your little girl grows up
    without Daddy's love,
    she may feel empty, and it's only because
    it's her daddy's love that she's looking for,
    don't send her away to another man's door.
Nobody else can do what you do,
    she just needs her daddy's love.

Have you given your little girl her daddy's love? If you haven't, please do. Go to her, and tell her that you love her. And that she is the most precious girl in the world to you. And what if you think it's too late? It's *never* too late. Even if she's twenty-seven, it wouldn't be too late. The song goes on with words of encouragement for those of you who may think it's too late:

And someday if you hear that her purity's is gone,
    she may have lost it tryin' to find
    what was missing at home.
Just let the heavenly Father
    heal where you fail,
He can forgive you and help you to give her
    the daddy's love that she's looking for,
    don't send her away to another man's door.

Nobody else can do what you do,
    she just needs her daddy's love.
You know it's true,
    she just need her daddy's love.

♡ ♡ ♡

Advice to My Friend

We may know what we as adults would share with a sexually involved teenager to encourage waiting. But what would one teenager share with another about waiting for sex? The following essay allows us to see what a certain teen's correspondence with his friend is like.

My friend, all I can do is share with you the pain and separation from our God that is due to my engaging in premarital sex; hopefully I can keep you from any further physical and spiritual damage.

The first experience I ever had was just passionate kissing with my first girl friend. It led to some problems. First, all I could think about was the next time we could get together; not so much to see her, but to kiss her and feel her body up close to mine. The other problem, since I was young, was that I was very possessive of her. This led to jealousy and pain when we broke up. I also began to think more of her than of God.

My next experiences with girls were all even more involved in trying to go "further" with them. There were a lot of frustrations and fears from both sides. Always before me was the thought of the girl and her body and how wonderful she felt held tight against me, how soft her body was, how nice her breasts felt, how I was just filled with an insatiable desire for her body. I was getting further from God and not caring because I had this new feeling that was just overwhelming.

I had my first experience with sexual intercourse with a girl that I really loved. I had even shared the gospel with her. We had fooled around with oral sex and a lot of kissing and petting. Finally on New Year's of 1981 we got into bed together and made love. It was a terrible experience. It was my first time, her first time, and what I thought then was the biggest tragedy of my life, the condom broke. Now that may sound funny but it wasn't. She and I were so worried that she was going to get pregnant that we cried and cried. I finally did the only thing I could do and that was to cry out to God for forgiveness and deliverance from our sin. Well, God proved faithful, but I didn't. I broke up the relationship on the grounds that I was not ready to be tied down yet. Who was I fooling? I was more than willing to involve myself physically with a woman in a way that God created only for marriage. Well, it really messed her up. The worst thing about it is that I really loused up for God. I had shared with her the gospel of love and told her that I loved her. Then when all was said and done I buzzed out. The reason for it was I had a taste of sex and wanted more. And I knew that because of my witness to her I couldn't stay with her and not marry.

Can't you see that once you get started with sex you will not want to stop? All you will do is crave more, more, more.

There's more to my story, more pain and hurt. I met a girl named Terri and we started going out. She had a reputation of "giving out." I felt kind of sorry for her because she was always abused. I wanted to show her what love was for. So we had a good, clean, friendly boyfriend-girl friend relationship.

Then finally I started to think about the things that had been said about her. I adopted the world's attitude and figured that I was mature enough and strong enough to deal with my emotions and my physical desires. We started to make love to each other. For her it was a liberation because it was someone who really cared about her for who she was, not because she was an "easy lay." For me it was what I wanted, a physical relationship with no marriage attached. We made love an average of four to seven times a week. We couldn't get enough of each other.

Finally she got tired of the relationship. No more challenge. Sex was still great, but who can live on sex? Well, I was completely devastated. I really loved her.

The real problem is that I was breaking God's commandments and joining myself to another person outside of the sanctification of wedlock. Can't you see that you and that person become a part of each other? Imagine losing an arm or a leg or even an eye. A part of the whole being that is you is gone.

Somehow, mysteriously, God has created a way to join yourself to a person through the physical that causes you to be joined to the person spiritually also. You begin to know things about her inner person that you never would have known otherwise.

God created sexual intercourse for the marriage so that we may leave and cleave, become one with our spouse, just as we will become one spiritually with Christ in heaven.

Seven months after we broke up she called me from another city to tell me that she was going to have a baby. Guess whose?

I was nineteen, she was seventeen. She had already arranged for the adoption and had the parents ready to accept on arrival. She had done it this way because she knew that I would want to keep the baby. Ensuing would be major custody battles on which family gets to keep the child. Also she couldn't stand having the child in the same town and having all her friends seeing it, and it not being hers to show. So what could I do? Drag my family in on it? Shatter the hopes of having a child for the people at the adoption agency? Mess up Terri's life here?

I had realized that I was receiving from God the rod of correction. I was really messed up knowing that I have a kid that I cannot even have. By the way, I had an 8-pound baby boy on October 2, 1984.

I just hope that God will open your eyes to what has happened to me. I am still haunted by the same desires but I have re-affirmed my stand with my Lord and He gives me strength to fight the pain and the intense passions that run through my body. I would not have to be going through these intense trials if I had kept to God's truth. Save your body for the woman God gives you. And then only involve yourself with her physically after you have been married, so that you can receive God's blessings, not His judgments.

I was a fool. You don't have to be. Pray about it. God will never fail you nor forsake you.

♡ ♡ ♡

Notes

Chapter 1
1. Ray and Anne Ortlund, "Never Too Late," *Parents and Teenagers,* Jay Kesler, gen. ed. with Ronald A. Beers (Wheaton: Victor Press, 1985), p. 91.
2. Evelyn Christenson, "Advice for Discouraged Parents," *Parents and Teenagers,* p. 74.
3. James Dobson, *Dr. Dobson Answers Your Questions,* (Wheaton: Tyndale House Publishers, 1982), pp. 465-66.

Chapter 7
1. Edgar S. Woody, M.D., "Teenage Pregnancy — Another Look," *Atlanta, Georgia, Medical Association Journal* (May 1979), Vol. 68, No. 5, pp. 400-402.

Chapter 9
1. "What World's Teens Are Saying," *U.S. News and World Report* (June 30, 1986), p. 68.
2. Marjory Roberts, "Adolescents: Teens of a Feather," *Psychology Today* (April 1986), p. 65.

Chapter 12
1. Josh McDowell, *The Secret of Loving* (San Bernardino, CA: Here's Life Publishers, 1985), pp. 38-39. Richard B. Austin, Jr., quoted from *How to Make It With Another Person* (New York: Macmillan Publishing Co., 1976), p. 93.
2. McDowell, *Secret;* David Augsburger quoted from *Freedom of Forgiveness* (Chicago: Moody Press, 1937), p. 87.

3. McDowell, *Secret;* David Augsburger quoted from *Caring Enough to Hear and Be Heard* (Ventura, CA: Regal Books, 1982), p. 104.

Chapter 21
1. Billy Graham, Foreword in *Parents and Teenagers,* Jay Kesler, gen. ed. with Ronald A. Beers (Wheaton: Victor Press, 1985), p. 17.

Chapter 22
1. Norman Wright, "The Art of Listening," *Parents and Teenagers,* J. Kesler, gen. ed., with Ronald A. Beers (Wheaton: Victor Books, 1985), p. 218.
2. Josh McDowell, *The Secret of Loving* (San Bernardino, CA: Here's Life Publishers, 1985).

Chapter 24
1. Janice Hopkins Tanne, "Aids: Is Anyone Safe?" *Readers Digest* (February 1986), vol. 128, pp. 60-64.
2. Lester R. Hibbard, M.D., *Questions Patients Most Often Ask Their Doctors* (New York: Bantam Books, 1983), n.p.
3. S. I. McMillen, *None of These Diseases* (Westwood, NJ: Revell, 1963), p. 46.
4. Anne Catherine Speckhard, "Psycho-Social Aspects of Stress Following Abortion" (doctoral dissertation, University of Minnesota, 1985), n.p.
5. Warren Wiersbe, *Be Challenged* (Chicago: Moody Press, 1982), pp. 39, 47.
6. Robert R. Bell, *Premarital Sex in a Changing Society* (Englewood Cliffs, NJ: Prentice-Hall, 1966), n.p.
7. Deborah Phillips, *Sexual Confidence* (Boston: Houghton Mifflin, 1980).
8. Sir Rabindranath Tagore, *Leadership* (Winter 1980), Vol. 1, No. 1, p. 117.

Resources

As you read this book you will become aware of a need for more information in various areas. Here is a list of resources that can be helpful to you.

Campbell, Ross. *How to Love a Teenager.* New York: New American Library, 1982.

Crabb, Lawrence J. *The Marriage Builder.* Grand Rapids: Zondervan Publishing House, 1982.

Dobson, James. *Preparing for Adolescence.* New York: Bantam Books, 1980.

Lewis, Paul. *Forty Ways to Teach Your Child Values.* Wheaton, IL: Tyndale House, 1985.

Mace, David R. *Christian Response to the Sexual Revolution.* Nashville: Abingdon Press, 1970.

McDowell, Josh. *Evidence for Joy.* Waco, TX: Word Books, 1984.

_____ . *Givers, Takers and Other Kinds of Lovers.* Wheaton: Tyndale House, 1985.

_____ . *His Image . . . My Image.* San Bernardino, CA: Here's Life Publishers, 1984.

_____ . *The Secret of Loving.* San Bernardino, CA: Here's Life Publishers, 1985.

_____ . *Why Wait? What You Need To Know About the Teen Sexuality Crisis.* San Bernardino, CA: Here's Life Publishers, 1987.

Stanley, Charles. *How to Keep Your Kids on Your Team.* Nashville: Oliver-Nelson, 1986.

Strommen, Merton P. *Five Cries of Youth.* New York: Harper & Row, 1974.

Strommen, Merton P. and Strommen, Irene. *Five Cries of Parents.* New York: Harper & Row, 1985.

Swindoll, Charles. *You and Your Child.* Nashville: Thomas Nelson, 1982.

Ziglar, Zig. *Raising Positive Kids in a Negative World.* Nashville: Thomas Nelson, 1985.

To obtain information on other books and on cassette tapes, films and videos, send for our complete resource catalog. Especially helpful for parents and teens will be the "Live, Laugh, Love" film series on love, sex and dating. For quickest response, write:

> Resource Catalog
> Josh McDowell Ministry
> P.O. Box 1000
> Dallas, TX 75221

Because very little top-notch material is available for the teens themselves, I am serving as series editor for three books that will help fill this need. They are:

Dating: Picking (and Being) a Winner
Sex: Desiring the Best
Love: Making It Last

Ask your bookstore for these important books, to be released soon by Here's Life Publishers. They will help our teenagers make some sense out of the present sexual/relationship dilemma. Barry St. Clair and Bill Jones, popular youth speakers, are doing an excellent job in pulling the books together.

LET'S STAY -IN- TOUCH!

If you have grown personally as a result of this material, we should stay in touch. You will want to continue in your Christian growth, and to help your faith become even stronger, our team is constantly developing new materials.

We are now publishing a monthly newsletter called 5 Minutes with Josh which will

1) tell you about those new materials as they become available
2) answer your tough questions
3) give creative tips on being an effective parent
4) let you know our ministry needs
5) keep you up to date on my speaking schedule (so you can pray).

If you would like to receive this publication, simply fill out the coupon below and send it in. By special arrangement 5 Minutes with Josh will come to you regularly — no charge.

Let's keep in touch!

Josh

☐ **Yes!** I want to receive the free subscription to **5 Minutes with JOSH**

_____
NAME

_____
ADDRESS

_____
CITY, STATE/ZIP

SLC-2024

Mail To:
Josh McDowell
c/o 5 Minutes with Josh
Campus Crusade for Christ
Arrowhead Springs
San Bernardino, CA 92414